STAPLEFORD HOUSE is the national conference and study centre of the Association of Christian Teachers. It offers Inservice Teacher Training Courses which provide professional training in developing a Christian perspective on education. Stapleford House also offers a school-based INSET service to primary and secondary schools providing support in the implementation of religious education and school worship. In conjunction with St John's College, Nottingham, Stapleford House runs a two year distance learning course in religious education leading to the award of a Diploma in Religious Education from Nottingham University. Also available is a distance learning course for non-teachers on leading school assemblies called 'Worship That Works'. For further information contact: Stapleford House Education Centre, ACT, Wesley Place, Stapleford, Nottingham NG9 8DP, Tel: (0602) 396270.

# Dedication

This book is dedicated to the memory of Pam Richardson, friend and mentor, and contributor to this publication who died on May 16th 1992.

# 52 IDEAS for SECONDARY CLASSROOM ASSEMBLIES

Edited by
**Janet King**
with Heike Schwarz

MONARCH
Tunbridge Wells

Copyright © Association of Christian Teachers 1992
The right of the Association of Christian Teachers to be
identified as author of this work has been asserted by them in
accordance with the Copyright, Design
and Patents Act 1988.

DISCLAIMER:
Every effort has been made to trace the owners of copyright
material, where this applies, and we hope that no copyright has
been infringed. Apology is made if the contrary is shown to be the
case, and correction will be made at the first opportunity.

First published 1992
Reprinted 1992

ISBN 1 85424 141 9

All rights reserved.
No part of this publication may be reproduced or
transmitted in any form or by any means, electronic
or mechanical, including photocopy, recording, or any
information storage and retrieval system, without
permission in writing from the publisher.

Unless otherwise indicated, biblical quotations are from the
Living Bible

**British Library Cataloguing in Publication Data.**
A catalogue record for this book is available from the British
Library.

Production and Printing in England
for MONARCH PUBLICATIONS
Owl Lodge, Langton Road, Speldhurst, Kent TN3 0NP
by Nuprint Ltd, Harpenden, Herts AL5 4SE.

# CONTENTS

Preface 7
Introduction 9
Contributors 17

1 A Helping Hand 20
2 Making Changes 23
3 Good Neighbours 27
4 Being Wrong 31
5 Jackstraws 35
6 Achievement 40
7 The Bible 44
8 Consequences 49
9 Worry 53
10 Be Yourself 59
11 The Disaster Movie 64
12 Selfishness 68
13 The Power Of Attraction 72
14 Dreams And Schemes 76
15 Jigsaw 80
16 Water 85
17 The Senses 89
18 Habits 93
19 Food And Feasting 98
20 It's A Miracle! 103
21 Don't Blame Me! 108
22 Getting To Know You 112

| 23 | Forgiveness | 116 |
| 24 | Two-Way Communication | 120 |
| 25 | A Time To Remember | 126 |
| 26 | Hope | 130 |
| 27 | Personal Values | 134 |
| 28 | Language Lines | 140 |
| 29 | Decisions | 145 |
| 30 | Misunderstandings | 151 |
| 31 | Dead Ends | 156 |
| 32 | Soap | 160 |
| 33 | Letters | 165 |
| 34 | It's A Mystery | 170 |
| 35 | Judging By Appearance | 174 |
| 36 | Money/Money/Money | 178 |
| 37 | Time | 183 |
| 38 | Words/Words/Words | 187 |
| 39 | Under The Influence | 191 |
| 40 | Pass It On | 196 |
| 41 | What's Your Name? | 202 |
| 42 | You Are Unique | 207 |
| 43 | Why Me? | 211 |
| 44 | I Believe | 215 |

## SPECIAL OCCASIONS

| 45 | Coping With Death | 220 |
| 46 | Harvest | 224 |
| 47 | Going To War (Remembrance Day) | 229 |
| 48 | Christmas | 234 |
| 49 | Easter 1—Good Friday | 241 |
| 50 | Easter 2—The Resurrection | 246 |
| 51 | Ascension | 250 |
| 52 | Pentecost | 254 |

## FURTHER SUGGESTIONS 259

# PREFACE

ALL THE TEACHERS I KNOW have difficulty in finding sufficient hours in the day to do everything that is required of them. Non-teachers may not always understand this, but anyone who goes into schools to lead assemblies or take the occasional lesson soon discovers that teaching is more than a nine-to-four job with long holidays!

With more and more demands being made on a teacher's time, one can understand the concern felt in some schools at the thought that they are required by law to provide a minimum of two hundred assemblies a year (ie one a day for forty weeks of the year). With time at a premium, planning and delivering daily acts of worship can seem to some like the proverbial straw that broke the camel's back.

There are resources around to help, but for many teachers, their assemblies are likely to be hastily put-together affairs rather than part of a planned exercise which represents a genuine attempt to stimulate serious thought on a wide range of topics.

This book is designed to help the thoughtful assembly leader by bringing together a collection of stimulating ideas and activities, which can be readily used and adapted according to individual needs.

In putting these outlines together, I have drawn on the ideas and work of a number of experienced assembly leaders, most of them teachers or schools' workers with a teaching background. A list of contributors may be found on pages 17-19. I am very grateful to them for their contributions. Without them, this book would not have been produced.

Finally, my special thanks to my research assistant, Heike Schwarz, who not only typed and juggled with the manuscript, but added the ideas for further research and contributed outlines of her own. Her tireless efforts have enabled me to bring this book to birth.

*Janet King*

Stapleford House Education Centre
Wesley Place
Stapleford
Nottingham
NG9 8DP.

# INTRODUCTION

During the course of my work as Religious Education and Worship Development Officer with the Association of Christian Teachers, I have had the opportunity to visit schools across the country and meet with people who organise and lead school assemblies. My observations and experience have led me to conclude that there has been a very mixed response by schools to the Education Reform Act's requirements concerning school worship.

Some schools seem to have given little thought to finding appropriate ways of responding to the legal requirements for daily worship, choosing to 'keep their heads down' in the hope of avoiding any 'flak'. Others have decided that what they were doing prior to the Act continues to be all they feel able to provide (ie in secondary schools this may only amount to one or two assemblies a week for most pupils). Yet others, four years on, claim they are 'still thinking about it'.

Many schools, however, have taken seriously the ERA's requirements and they are attempting to provide a programme of daily assemblies which reflect the fact that the majority of their acts of worship should be 'wholly or mainly of a broadly Christian character'. They have also taken into account the circumstances relating to the family background of pupils as well as the ages and aptitudes of the pupils in their charge. This has led to a variety of assembly programmes, some of which allow for separate acts of worship for different religious groups in the school, while others have opted for a programme which keeps pupils together without anyone feeling that their own faith is being compromised or that their personal beliefs are being undermined. Some schools have decided to combine both these approaches.

Whatever the response, there has been widespread approval of the new flexibility over timing which allows for worship to be held at any time during the school day. There has been some relief that it has been recognised that schools find it physically impossible to accommodate the whole school for a single act of collective worship. On the other hand, there is some anxiety about the continued use of the word 'worship' in the school context, and the required 'Christian' content.

It is not my purpose to discuss the ERA's requirements here, or to go into any detailed comment on the problems or possibilities it has created. Anyone requiring this kind of detailed information and analysis of present law or guidance on practical issues relating to leading assemblies, should refer to my book *Leading Worship in Schools*.[1]

In the seventies and eighties many schools moved away from a Christian pattern, choosing instead to hold largely secular or multi-faith types of assembly. Some schools, faced with the problem of insufficient staff willing to organise or lead assemblies, gave them up altogether. It is not surprising then that the new Act's requirements for school worship have prompted some cries for help particularly in the form of fresh resources.

# THE AIM OF THIS BOOK

This book is a direct response to this need. It is designed for the busy teacher looking for stimulating, practical ideas which can be used with the minimum of preparation. It contains 52 themes, all of which provide a range of ideas and activities together with further suggestions for development. Every outline includes some reference to Christian belief or practice with the intention of providing a clear understanding of some of the tenets of the Christian faith. Within each assembly outline, a range of activities is provided so that teachers and their pupils have the freedom to choose only those with which they feel comfortable, thus allowing them the opportunity to be involved without compromising their personal beliefs. All outlines and activities can also be tailored according to the time available for daily worship.

The aim of this book is to present pupils with material which encourages personal enquiry. Worship in the school context must be of the 'collective' variety and not 'corporate'. Corporate worship requires a body of believers capable of responding and participating in the same way. Collective worship allows for a variety of responses and recognises the fact that schools must cater for a community in which people hold various religious and non-religious commitments. This is an important distinction.

Nevertheless, the fact that the 1988 ERA uses only the specific term 'act of worship' rather than 'assembly' means that every school and every individual teacher needs to cogitate on the attendant implications. Although some pupils may have little or no previous personal spiritual experience upon which they can draw, it is my hope that these outlines will offer them the opportunity not only to approach the threshold of Christian worship, but on occasions lead some pupils beyond the threshold and into a place where they can experience worship for themselves.

For this reason, this book should be seen as a tool which offers teachers the opportunity to take a fresh and exciting look at their assembly programme. Most of the schools in the maintained sector have moved away from the idea that school assemblies should be mini-versions of the type of worship found in church amongst a group of committed believers, and so alternative models have been sought.

## PLANNING AN ASSEMBLY PROGRAMME

The approach which prompted me into writing and collecting the material for this book, has been the planned programme which seeks to deliver the Act's requirements through a combination of 'hall', year group and tutor group assemblies. In most cases where this programme has been introduced, a list of themes for each week of the term is prepared, usually by the person in charge of organising and coordinating the assemblies, or by a planning team. Sometimes, helpful material on those themes is also provided but, in some cases, little or no help is given with regard to how the theme is to be tackled, and no real guidance offered on how to handle the required Christian element. I hope this book will help to fill this gap.

When planning an assembly programme, most head teachers will want to involve other members of staff and probably delegate responsibility for the overall supervision of the programme to a deputy or another experienced member of staff. For the programme to succeed, it will require time, effort and money to resource it. It is also wise to ensure that all staff have the opportunity to voice their opinions and make their contribution to the debate. A workable plan involving the staff will need their support. This is more likely to be given if they are consulted from the start.

Every school needs to develop its own programme so that it is seen not only to meet the legal requirements, but is tailored to the unique individual needs of the school. What may be appropriate in one situation may be quite inappropriate in another. If your school has not thought through its worship programme, the following model may be helpful in setting the process in motion:

## A POSSIBLE MODEL FOR PLANNING A SCHOOL WORSHIP PROGRAMME

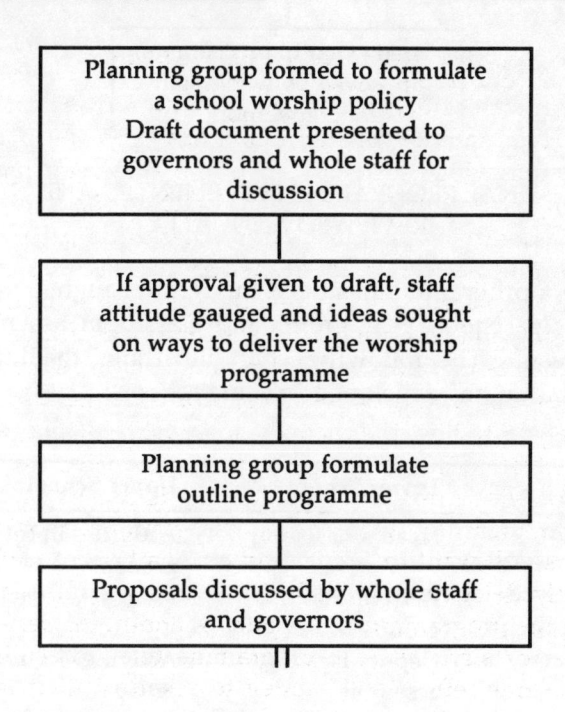

```
┌─────────────────────────────────────┐
│   Planning group formed to formulate │
│      a school worship policy         │
│     Draft document presented to      │
│    governors and whole staff for     │
│              discussion              │
└─────────────────────────────────────┘
                  │
┌─────────────────────────────────────┐
│    If approval given to draft, staff │
│    attitude gauged and ideas sought  │
│    on ways to deliver the worship    │
│              programme               │
└─────────────────────────────────────┘
                  │
┌─────────────────────────────────────┐
│      Planning group formulate        │
│         outline programme            │
└─────────────────────────────────────┘
                  │
┌─────────────────────────────────────┐
│   Proposals discussed by whole staff │
│            and governors             │
└─────────────────────────────────────┘
```

**IDENTIFY POTENTIAL LEADERS**

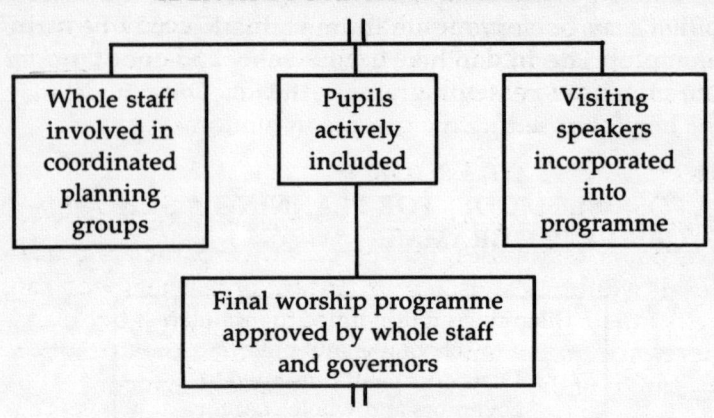

- Whole staff involved in coordinated planning groups
- Pupils actively included
- Visiting speakers incorporated into programme

Final worship programme approved by whole staff and governors

FINAL PROGRAMME IMPLEMENTED AND REVIEWED ANNUALLY

Where a programme has been thought through, a system of whole school, year group and classroom assemblies may result. The following chart illustrates the kind of pattern that has developed in some schools:

| Day | Lower School | Upper School |
|---|---|---|
| MON | Head's Assembly | Activities in tutor groups |
| TUES | Activities in tutor groups | Head's Assembly |
| FRI | Deputy Head's assembly | Activities in tutor groups |
| WEDS THURS | Year group assemblies on a rota whilst other years have activities in tutor groups ||
| Special Occasions | Whole school celebration of special events (ie Christmas, Easter, etc) ||

Where this kind of plan is implemented, this book offers a range of themes that can be introduced in a main assembly, explored in the year assembly and developed in the tutor group assembly.

## HOW TO USE THIS BOOK

Where a school has a planned programme which involves classroom assemblies, this book will be particularly useful. It will be best used with a team of teachers who can select their themes from those outlined in the book and develop a programme which will suit their own situation by building their ideas into the outlines provided.

The range of topics allowed some choice in the themes to be used, and the options and ideas contained in each outline allow for some choice within the topics selected. All the themes seek to provide the teacher with a Christian focus within the items offered, but some outlines will be seen to be more specifically Christian than others. It will be up to individual schools, and the teachers involved, to decide how to use these in order to achieve a balance appropriate to their school.

This book may also be used in conjunction with other material as deemed appropriate taking into account the religious or secular background of the pupils concerned. My purpose is to provide assembly leaders with ideas that will fulfil the Christian requirements of the Act, whilst giving teachers room for manoeuvre bearing in mind legal and educational responsibilities.

What is offered to pupils should be recorded in a clear and concise way so that there can be some attempt to monitor what is done, and build in a system of checks and balances. In this way it can be seen that in the course of any one term, a clear and genuine attempt is made to deliver a programme of assemblies where Christianity will feature regularly in the classroom setting as well as in the main assemblies.

Such a planned programme also allows for visitors to be used on some occasions. Every effort should be made when inviting outside speakers into the school to ensure that they understand the educational framework within which they are being invited to contribute, and are known to be capable of presenting their material in an acceptable way. With this in mind the school may wish to prepare some guidelines for visitors, or refer them to my *Leading Worship In Schools*.[2] The ACT directory of visitors available to support schools in worship, the curriculum and voluntary groups entitled *Now Who Can We Ask?*, is another valuable resource available to teachers wanting detailed information about Christians (locally and nationally) who are available to go into schools.[3]

Finally, whatever the arrangements made by the school, it is my hope that this material will help in providing pupils with a balanced, legal and educationally stimulating programme of daily worship.

**FOOTNOTES**

[1] Janet King, *Leading Worship In Schools* (Monarch/CiE: Eastbourne, 1990), ISBN 1 85424 077 3.
[2] *op cit*.
[3] Janet King/Heike Schwarz, *Now Who Can We Ask?* (Stapleford House Education Centre: Nottingham, 1991), ISBN 0 9516537 1 7.

# CONTRIBUTORS

**DIANE BURROWS** is a housewife and mother who, in her spare time, takes assemblies regularly in both primary and secondary schools in the Nottingham area. She is the Coordinator of her church's 'A-Team' which is a group of twelve people who go into schools to lead assemblies.

**MARGARET COOLING** was until recently a Co-Director of ACT's Education Centre and is herself the author of several assembly books. She has a wide experience of teaching and leading assemblies as she has worked in both the primary and secondary sectors.

**SALLY LYNCH** has taught for nine years and is currently Head of RE at St Bede's Comprehensive Church School, Cambridge. She is also an experienced assembly leader and co-ordinates the assemblies in her present school.

**PETER McCAUSLAND** is Head of RE at Parkhill High School in Antrim, Northern Ireland. He regularly leads whole-school and form-based assemblies and is also a member of the RE Drafting Group for the NI Education Reform proposals.

**BOB MILLIKEN** is an experienced assembly leader and Head of the RE Department at Crofton Secondary School in Hampshire.

He is also the Youth Pastor at Paulsgrove Baptist Church and a co-worker with the Scripture Union Link Up Scheme.

**RICHARD MORRISON** is a full-time Schools' Worker with the CROPS Trust (Christian Options in Peterborough Schools). He first started leading assemblies in 1971 and has been a Youth Pastor and a Schools' Worker with Scripture Union.

**KEITH PENTELOW** spent four years as a Youth Worker serving the Anglican and Methodist Churches in the parish of All Saints Thorpe Acre with Dishley in Loughborough. In this role he spent half of his time working with local schools taking RE lessons and assemblies. Since July 1991 he has been employed as Youth Minister by two Anglican churches in Chilwell, Nottingham.

**PAM RICHARDSON** was Senior Teacher at Loxford High School in Ilford, Essex, and had been Head of RE and Head of Business Studies. She had over thirty years of teaching and assembly leading experience.

**HEIKE SCHWARZ** is a qualified RE teacher who has worked with ACT since September 1988. She is the compiler of a comprehensive bibliography of education materials written from a Christian perspective. She currently works as a research assistant to the Development Officer and regularly leads assemblies in local schools.

**TED SKINNER** is Head of Upper School and Head of RE at Chadwell Heath High School. He has a wide experience of teaching and leading assemblies having worked in both secondary and junior high schools. He is also an elder at his local Brethren Fellowship and a youth leader.

**MARTIN SWEET** is an associate Scripture Union worker supported by the Spinnaker Trust which was set up in 1986. He taught for nine years in a Beckenham Comprehensive School where he became Head of Sixth Year. He takes assemblies regularly and also visits local schools with his *IN TIME* Drama Group.

**MARY SMITH** has taught in both primary and secondary schools and is currently Head of RE and Coordinator of daily worship at Kirk Hallam Community School in Derbyshire.

**SYLVIA VINCENT** is an experienced assembly leader who also writes assembly material. She has taught a wide range of age groups and worked in Germany and the Far East. She is currently Head of an infant school in the Bristol area.

My special thanks to Malcolm Laverty for the cartoons on pages 38, 62, 104, 124, 138, 147, 153, 168, 200, 203, 217 and 239 and to Paul Richardson for the illustrations on pages 81 and 179.

# 1

## THEME

# A Helping Hand
### (First week of term)

**AIM**

To show that it is important for a community to work together in giving and receiving.

**INTRODUCTION**

Get all the pupils together in a circle facing inwards. Everyone is to stretch out their hands and grasp hold of any two other hands from the other side. Having done this they are in a knot. The whole group must cooperate now to untangle the knot without letting go of any hands.[1] Explain that the purpose of the exercise is to illustrate the importance of working together. We all need help from others at certain times in our lives, both in school and in life.

**OPTIONS AND IDEAS**

A. Have a chocolate marshmallow (or something similarly edible), a knife and fork, each attached to the end of a broom handle, and with some red tape woven around the handles at the other end. Invite someone who likes marshmallows to come forward and eat one. But there is a condition: they have to use the knife and fork and hold them only by the taped handle. The person will try many ways but without success. Ask the rest of the class what is needed and work towards the answer: it needs another person to come, do the cutting, and feed the one who couldn't reach.[2] Make the point that at the start of a new term, it is good to remind ourselves that we will all get more out of life in school if we 'work together'.

B. Talk about the difficulties involved in trying to help people who don't want to be helped. Some people think they can do everything themselves without help from anyone. To illustrate this, refer to the story of Winnie the Pooh, Piglet and Rabbit when they play the game 'Poohsticks' and find Eeyore floating in the river.[3] Ask: 'How did Eeyore react to being rescued?' Point out that he resented it, claiming that he saved himself.

C. In pairs let pupils discuss and write down how they might need help at different times (eg with homework, when they suffer a bereavement in the family, etc) and what kind of help would be appropriate.

D. Look up the story of Jesus washing the feet of his friends as recounted in the story in John 13:1–15. Get pupils to imagine themselves as one of the disciples present that night. Ask them to record the events and their feelings about the evening in diary form.

E. Suggest that some members of the group might like to think quietly about the following prayer and the importance of serving others and of letting others help you. A helping hand works both ways—giving and receiving.

Brother, let me be your servant,
Let me be as Christ to you;
Pray that I may have the grace
To let you be my servant, too.[4]

## IDEAS FOR DEVELOPMENT

Plan some inter-house or tutor group activities to raise money for a community charity project.

Divide into small groups of three or four. Each group has to work together to form a letter on the floor, using their bodies. Start with simple letters such as O, H, L, T and then move to more complicated ones such as M, W, N, and R.

**FOOTNOTES**

[1] 'Untangling' in: Ros Aspinall, *CreActivity—Creative Workshops For World Concern* (Y CARE International: 640 Forest Road, London E17 3DZ, 1988), ISBN 0 948810 01 7, p 45.

[2] Adapted from: Michael Botting (ed), *For All The Family—Illustrated Talks For Family Services* (Kingsway: Eastbourne, 1984), ISBN 0 86065 314 5, pp 131-132.

[3] 'In Which Pooh Invents A New Game And Eeyore Joins In' in: A. A. Milne, *The House At Pooh Corner* (Methuen Children's Books: London, 1928, reprinted 1982), pp 90-99.

[4] Richard Gillard, 'The Servant Song'—verse 1' in: Betty Pulkingham/Mimi Farra (ed), *Cry Hosanna* (Hodder & Stoughton: Sevenoaks, 1980), ISBN 0 340 25159 X, p 117. © 1977 Scripture in Song.

# 2

## THEME

# Making Changes

**AIM**
   i) To consider how much power we have to change ourselves or things around us.
   ii) To think about Christian belief in the power of Jesus to transform people.

**INTRODUCTION**
Some pupils will have read *The Voyage Of The Dawn Treader* by C. S. Lewis or seen the BBC production or video of the story. Those who have may recall the incident when Eustace was changed into a dragon by his greed and finally freed by Aslan who scrapes away his dragon coat. Tell or read this extract from the book or show the relevant clip from the video to introduce the subject.[1] Alternatively, if you are familiar with the Teenage Mutant Ninja Turtles stories you can prepare your own jar of 'mutating gel' to use as a visual aid to a brief summary of the basic plot.[2]

## OPTIONS AND IDEAS

A. Use the following questions to draw out the significance of Eustace's story: (a) 'Why do you think Eustace was turned into a dragon?' (b) 'What effect did this have on him as a person?' (c) 'How did he get changed back again?' (d) 'What lessons might be learnt from this whole experience?'

B. Take up the idea behind the Teenage Mutant Ninja Turtles stories that they were mutant/humanoid forms who became like the last living creature they touched before being covered in the gel. Ask: 'What would be the last creature you would like to touch if you could be changed in this way?' 'Why?'

C. Give pupils time to reflect quietly on the list of positive and negative characteristics listed below. Ask them to think which of these really apply to them at the moment, and which they would like to be known for:

| loving ☐ | selfish ☐ | kind ☐ |
| envious ☐ | caring ☐ | gentle ☐ |
| responsible ☐ | spiteful ☐ | mean ☐ |
| cheerful ☐ | considerate ☐ | hot tempered ☐ |

D. Explain that Christians believe that Jesus has the power to change lives. A Bible story that illustrates this is the account of Paul's life-changing experience on the road to Damascus. Familiarise pupils with this story in Acts 9:1–25, then read this extract from a modern-day story about change which is recounted in an interview with a teenager called Christine:

> Christine, working on a job creation scheme at the time of the interview, went into great detail about her family relationships.
> They think it is fantastic how much I've changed. They can hardly believe it. Whereas once they

couldn't trust me at all, not even as far as they could throw me, now when I say it's the truth they believe it is the truth. They have actually said how different I am to them, and although my dad does not believe in Christianity, he says that whatever made me change is great.[3]

Ask if anyone has had an experience that resulted in a change of some kind in their life. Ask: 'If you could change something about yourself or your life, what would it be?'

E. Look at the story of the blind man:

As he [Jesus] was walking along, he saw a man blind from birth. Then he spat on the ground and made mud from the spittle and smoothed the mud over the blind man's eyes, and told him, 'Go and wash in the Pool of Siloam'. So the man went where he was sent and washed and came back seeing!
The Pharisees investigated this man's healing and questioned him. He told them how it happened and said: 'If this man Jesus were not from God, he couldn't do it.' But when the Pharisees heard that, they threw him out.
When Jesus heard what had happened, he found the man and said, 'Do you believe in the Messiah?' 'Who is he, sir, for I want to.' 'You have seen him,' Jesus said, 'and he is speaking to you!' 'Yes, Lord,' the man said, 'I believe!' And he worshipped Jesus.
(Abridged from John 9:1,6–7,35–38).

Suggest that it might be fun to think of the 'clay' as 'mutating gel'! Discuss what really changed this man: the 'clay' or this man's faith in Jesus.

F. If appropriate, use the following prayer in a time of quiet reflection:

Lord, when I look at myself and the negative aspects

of my character, I long for transformation. Jesus, please touch my life and change those aspects of my personality that are not pleasing to you. Amen.

## IDEAS FOR DEVELOPMENT

Find out about some contemporary Christians who claim their lives of violence and hatred were changed dramatically when they became Christians (eg Fred Lemon, Brian Greenaway, Nicky Cruz).[4]

**FOOTNOTES:**

[1] C. S. Lewis, *The Voyage Of The Dawn Treader* (Fontana/Collins: London, 1980), pp 66-87.
C. S. Lewis, *The Chronicles Of Narnia—The Voyage Of The Dawn Treader* (BBC Enterprises: London, 1990). A BBC TV production, available now on video in some local video shops. Duration: 109 minutes.

[2] *Teenage Mutant Ninja Turtles*. Available in most local video shops.

[3] Philip May/David Day, *Teenage Beliefs* (Lion Publishing: Oxford, 1991), ISBN 0 7459 1963 4, p 127.

[4] Anne Tyler, *Bitter...Sweet—The Fred Lemon Story* (Marshall Pickering: Basingstoke, 1987), ISBN 0 551 01403 2.
'Life Situation: Fred Lemon' in: Linda Smith, *All About Living—2* (Lion Publishing: Tring, 1986), ISBN 0 7459 1161 7, pp 57-60.
Brian Greenaway/Clive Langmead, *Inside* (Lion Publishing: Tring, 1985), ISBN 0 85648 842 9.
Nicky Cruz/Jamie Buckingham, *Run Baby Run* (Hodder & Stoughton: Sevenoaks, 1968), ISBN 0 340 14958 2.
R. J. Owen, *The Killer Who Cried—The Story Of Nicky Cruz* (Religious and Moral Education Press: Exeter, 1980), ISBN 0 08 024958 2.

# 3

## THEME

# Good Neighbours

**AIM**
To explore the concept of the good neighbour.

**INTRODUCTION**
Prepare the ten 'Neighbours' cards as follows:

N = notices
E = enthusiastic
I = inquiring
G = good listener
H = humour
B = big-hearted
O = open
U = unbiased
R = ready
S = special

Make the cards with the letter, ie [ N ]

on one side, and the explanation, ie

| NOTICES | on the other.

Complete as above using all the letters of 'Neighbours'.

Invite ten pupils to come to the front to hold up the prepared letter cards. Explain that each card indicates one aspect of a good neighbour.

## OPTIONS AND IDEAS

A. The ten cards should be held with the letters facing the 'audience' so that they spell out the word neighbours. One at a time, the pupils then turn their card around to display the word written on the other side. Talk about the positive aspects of each word as it is shown, eg notices—notices that the milk has not been taken in and thinks 'Is that neighbour ill?'

B. Study this extract which gives a biblical view on the subject of neighbours:

> The Old Testament laws include many about 'the neighbour'. The neighbour is the person next door or along the street, the brother-Israelite, the fellow-citizen or, at a pinch, the visitor who has settled down with you for a while.
> Such a person has to be respected as you would respect yourself. He must be loved in the day-to-day details of life. You are not to steal his wife, life, property or children. You are not to defraud him in trade, withhold his wages, oppress him with exorbitant rates of interest, curse him if he is deaf or trip him up if he is blind. You are not secretly to shift his boundary stone to gain extra land, nor give false evidence against him in court, nor even covet anything that rightfully belongs to him.

> The neighbour laws were just one of the ways in which Israel was to be 'holy' like her God. The community flourished when each person loved his neighbour as himself. When everyone was set against his neighbour, it signalled the breakdown of society.
>
> The laws on neighbours were well known. The issue in Jesus' day was about who was to count as a neighbour. Where to draw the line was a matter of intense debate. Most agreed the term included the fellow-countryman and the convert. Some argued that personal enemies did not count, and others taught that you had a duty to push 'heretics, informers and renegades' into the ditch, not pull them out. Pharisees, not surprisingly, excluded non-Pharisees. No one dreamed that Gentiles could ever be neighbours, of course. And there was a saying that 'a piece of bread given by a Samaritan is more unclean than swine's flesh'. Everyone continued to define the exclusion zone.[1]

C. Explain that when Jesus was asked the question: 'Who is my neighbour?' he refused to be drawn into the 'old' debate in the terms outlined in the above extract, but chose instead to answer the question with a story. Read or tell the story of the Good Samaritan from Luke 10:29–37, and explain that Samaritans were regarded by Jews in Jesus' time as an ungodly race who were even worse than other Gentiles (non-Jews). They despised them and used the word 'Samaritan' as an obscene insult. This was why the scribe used the phrase 'the one who showed mercy' to describe the neighbour as he would not have wanted to 'soil his lips' by uttering the word 'Samaritan'. Nevertheless, Jesus used the story to illustrate who was the true neighbour according to and even beyond the Jewish Law.[2] Provoke discussion of this parable by asking questions like: 'Is my neighbour just the person who lives next door?' Show that all the people we have contact with are our neighbours in the sense implied in the story, even our enemies.

D. Brainstorm pupils for ideas on how they can be a good neighbour or a better neighbour: (1) in school, (2) at home, (3) in the community, and (4) in the world.

E. Hire/borrow the soundstrip *The Ballad Of Vincent And Kevin*.[3] It is a modern version of the 'Good Samaritan' story.

F. Discuss practical ways in which they as individuals and as a group can be better neighbours (eg a class effort to raise money for a worthy cause or organising some sort of Christmas entertainment for neighbours of the school, etc).

G. Younger pupils may enjoy singing: 'When I Needed A Neighbour'.[4]

**IDEAS FOR DEVELOPMENT**
Watch the local press for stories about good neighbours.

**FOOTNOTES**

[1] 'The Neighbour' in: Robin Keeley (ed), *The Message Of The Bible* (Lion Publishing: Tring, 1988), ISBN 0 85648 917 4, p 40.

[2] *ibid* p 41.
Herbert Sundemo, *Dictionary Of Bible Times* (Scripture Union: London, 1979), ISBN 0 85421 538 7, p 171.

[3] *The Ballad Of Vincent And Kevin* (Scripture Union, 130 City Road, London EC1V 2NJ). Available as video or soundstrip: six minutes. Script reprinted in RE textbook: Linda Smith, *All About Living 3* (Lion Publishing: Tring, 1986), ISBN 0 7459 1162 5, p 39.

[4] Sydney Carter, 'When I Needed A Neighbour' in: Peter Horrobin/ Greg Leavers (compilers), *Junior Praise* (Marshall Pickering: Basingstoke, 1986), ISBN 0 551 01293 5, pp 480-481.

# 4

## THEME

# Being Wrong

**AIM**

To consider some of the effects of being proved wrong and the importance of responding positively to truth.

**INTRODUCTION**

Hand round a jar of dried peas. Ask pupils to write down how many peas they think there are in the bottle.

**OPTIONS AND IDEAS**

A. Allow each pupil about fifteen seconds to write down their estimated number. Before you reveal the correct answer ask some questions like: (a) 'Can we all be right?' (b) 'Can we come to a consensus of opinion?' (c) 'Is there a scientific or mathematical formula we can use to get the number right?' (d) 'How do we get the right answer?' Explain that the game originator is the only one who really knows the correct answer. And the true answer is...

B. Ask pupils to share their reactions to finding out the correct number. If they were in the wrong, did they feel their answer was near enough—did the revelation of the correct number make them feel devalued as a person? Explore the idea of the importance of responding in a positive way when we are shown to be wrong or when the truth is revealed. Pupils may be able to provide stories about 'being a bad loser' to illustrate the point.

C. Point out that one cannot always expect to win or to be right in life. Here are some examples of people who time has shown to be wrong about something:

> 'Far too noisy, my dear Mozart. Far too many notes.'—The Emperor Ferdinand after the first performance of *The Marriage Of Figaro*.

> 'Stanley Matthews lacks the big match temperament. He will never hold down a regular first team place in top class soccer.'—Unsigned football writer when Matthews, the future captain of England, made his debut at the age of seventeen.

> 'Flight by machines heavier than air is unpractical and insignificant, if not utterly impossible'—Simon Newcomb (1835-1909). The first flight by the Wright Brothers eighteen months afterwards did not affect his opinion.

> 'We don't like their sound. Groups of guitars are on the way out.'—Decca Recording Company when turning down the Beatles in 1962. (The group was also turned down by Pye, Columbia, and HMV.)

> 'Rembrandt is not to be compared in the painting of character with our extraordinarily gifted English artist, Mr Rippingille'—John Hunt (1775-1848).

'You will never amount to very much'—A Munich Schoolmaster to Albert Einstein, aged 10.[1]

Make the point that people are often wrong in what they say so we should not be too upset when we make mistakes. The important thing is to learn from them and not be afraid to admit when we are shown to be wrong. This is a sign of strength rather than a sign of weakness.

D. Draw up a list of situations where being wrong could have serious implications, eg a doctor giving the wrong prescription, an electrical system being wrongly wired (ie like the signalling system in the railway). Discuss the question of when being wrong is something that can't be helped and comes out of ignorance, and when it is the result of a lack of concern, or a wilful action.

E. Some people reach a point in their lives where they feel that they need to rethink many ideas and beliefs they have held in the past. C. S. Lewis, a notable literary scholar and Christian writer of *The Chronicles of Narnia* records in his book *Surprised By Joy* how he turned from atheism to belief in the existence of a god, and eventually to Christianity.[2] After reading the extract ask pupils for their reactions to it:

> You must picture me alone in that room in Magdalen, night after night, feeling, whenever my mind lifted even for a second from my work, the steady, unrelenting approach of him whom I so earnestly desired not to meet. That which I greatly feared had at last come upon me. In the Trinity term of 1929 I gave in, and admitted that God was God, and knelt and prayed: perhaps, that night, the most dejected and reluctant convert in all England.

F. Explain that Christians believe that through the Bible

the unseen God has revealed truth—truth about himself, truth about human nature, truth about the universe. But that does not mean he has revealed everything there is to be known. The Bible also declares that Jesus not only spoke the truth or showed the way to truth but that he *is* 'the Truth'—a liberating truth:

> Jesus told him, 'I am the Way—yes, and the Truth and the Life. No one can get to the Father except by means of me' (John 14:6).

> Jesus said to them, 'You are truly my disciples if you live as I tell you to, and you will know the truth, and the truth will set you free' (John 8:31-32).

Think about the different ways in which people reacted to these statements of Jesus. Invite pupils to reflect quietly on the real meaning of Jesus' words.

**IDEAS FOR DEVELOPMENT**
> Find out about other famous people who changed their beliefs such as Sadhu Sundar Singh, Doreen Irvine, Rabindranath R. Maharaj, Bilquis Sheikh.[3]

**FOOTNOTES**

[1] 'The Art Of Being Wrong' in: Stephen Pile, *The Book Of Heroic Failures* (Macdonald Futura Publishers: London, 1980), pp 213-216. Reproduced by permission of Rogers, Coleridge & White Ltd.

[2] C. S. Lewis, *Surprised By Joy* (Fount/Collins: Glasgow, 1955), pp 182-183.

[3] 'Sadhu Sundar Singh—Who Could Not Forget Tibet' In: Phyllis Thompson, *Dawn In The East* (Marshall Pickering: London, 1990), ISBN 0 551 02018 0, pp 14-25.
Doreen Irvine, *From Witchcraft To Christ* (Concordia Press: Boreham Wood, 1973), ISBN 570 00070 X.
Rabindranath R. Maharaj/Dave Hunt, *Death Of A Guru* (Hodder & Stoughton: Sevenoaks, 1977), ISBN 0 340 22346 4.
Bilquis Sheikh/Richard Schneider, *I Dared To Call Him Father* (Kingsway: Eastbourne, 1978), ISBN 0 86065 049 9.

# 5

## THEME
# Jackstraws

**AIM**
- i) To create an awareness of interdependence and to counteract extreme individualism.
- ii) To provoke thought on the Christian view of the church as a corporate body.

**INTRODUCTION**

Play a game of 'Jackstraws' (with about twenty drinking straws). Hold them six inches above the desk before dropping them. Invite two or three volunteers to remove as many straws as they can without disturbing any others.[1]

**OPTIONS AND IDEAS**

A. Use the game to show that by touching one straw it is easy to affect many others. This is true for people, too, in that we are interdependent. What affects one person affects others: 'No man is an island, entire of itself: every man is a piece of the continent, a part of the main... Any man's death diminishes me, because I am involved in mankind.'[2] Give two examples of negative impact on each other (eg one pupil disrupting a lesson impedes everyone's progress) and some positive examples (eg a few people working hard to raise money for a charity may enthuse others).

B. Explain that Christians see each individual person as part of a 'body'. Each has a different function, but each is necessary. The following Bible passage can be read to illustrate this point:

> Yes, the body has many parts, not just one part. If the foot says, 'I am not a part of the body because I am not a hand,' that does not make it any less a part of the body. And what would you think if you heard an ear say, 'I am not part of the body because I am only an ear, and not an eye'? Would that make it any less a part of the body? Suppose the whole body were an eye—then how would you hear? Or if your whole body were just one big ear, how could you smell anything? But that isn't the way God has made us. He has made many parts for our bodies and has put each part just where he wants it.
> So God has put the body together in such a way that extra honour and care are given to those parts that might otherwise seem less important. This makes for happiness among the parts, so that the parts have the same care for each other that they do for themselves. If one part suffers, all parts suffer with it, and if one part is honoured, all the parts are glad. Now here is what I am trying to say: All of you together are the one body of Christ and each one of you is a separate and necessary part of it (1 Corinthians 12:14-18,24b-27).

C. Ask if anyone saw any of the Challenge Anneka programmes. Explain that she would be given various challenges—for example she was set the task of renovating a Rumanian orphanage and improving the horrific conditions of the children (some of whom were mentally handicapped and had serious medical conditions). Anyone who saw the programme will be able to recall that many volunteers with a variety of skills came forward to help in the challenge. The result was that the job was eventually completed because each person contributed and fulfilled their particular function.

D. Play the game 'Interdependence'.[3] You will need cord or ribbon, scissors and a pitcher full of water for it. Players have their left hand tied to the right hand of the player on the left, and their right hand tied to the left hand of the player on their right. The tied-up group then distributes a drink of water (directly into the mouth) to each of its members or performs some other task which its members wish to attempt. Warning: This game can be a bit messy and wet! You can play it with the whole class, or alternatively, split your class into two groups: one group plays the game, the other group watches carefully how well the group is cooperating and reports back at the end of the game. Then swap over.

E. Talk about the importance of working together as a team. Discuss ways in which team work plays an important role in school situations (eg working in a group project, sports activities, school concert, school play).

**IDEAS FOR DEVELOPMENT**

Discuss ways in which the class could work together on a project which would allow each person the opportunity to display their particular abilities and talents.

Make a collage of a person made out of pictures from only one part of the body (eg ears).

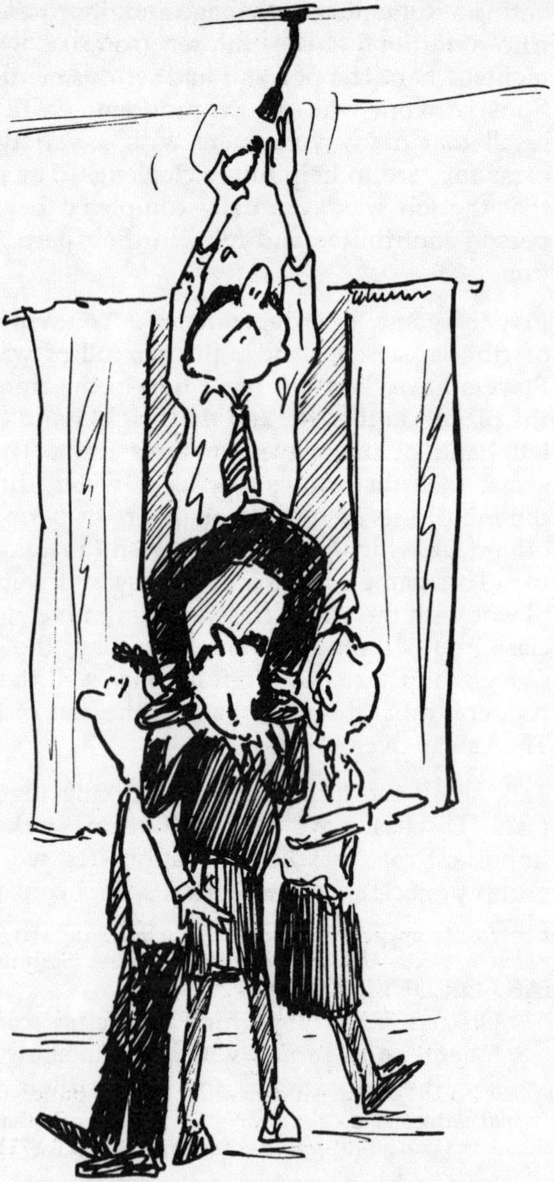

Do a project on pollution (eg the Gulf oil slick, nuclear accidents like Chernobyl). Show how these have affected various countries.

**FOOTNOTES**

[1] This originally appeared in a different context in: Margaret Cooling, *Love And Sex—Making Responsible Choices* (Scripture Union: London, 1989), ISBN 0 86201 392 5, p 28.

[2] John Donne, 'No Man Is An Island' in: Anthony P. Castle, *Quotes & Anecdotes—An Anthology For Preachers & Teachers* (Kevin Mayhew: Bury St Edmunds 1979), ISBN 0 905725 69 7, p 239.

[3] Adapted from: 'Interdependence' in: Susan Butler (compiler), *Non-Competitive Games For People Of All Ages* (Bethany House Publishers: Minneapolis/Minnesota 1986), ISBN 0 87123 812 8, p 133.

# 6

## THEME

# Achievement

**AIM**
  i) To show that to achieve something really worthwhile one must be prepared for some sacrifices.
  ii) To think about what motivates Christians.

**INTRODUCTION**
  Show or talk about two or three personal achievements—a trophy, certificate or a prize. Ask pupils to indicate if they have ever won a prize or certificate for something.

**OPTIONS AND IDEAS**

A. Make the point that everyone enjoys achieving some ambition, fulfilling a goal or winning a prize. Offer the opportunity for three pupils to win a prize today (eg a Cadbury's Cream Egg each!). Ask the following questions (update and apply as appropriate): (a) 'Who was awarded the Templeton Award and the Nobel Peace Prize for her work amongst the homeless and dying of

Calcutta?' (Answer: Mother Teresa). (b) 'Which English snooker player has won every major honour in the game (including the World Championship six times) since turning professional in 1978?' (Answer: Steve Davis). (c) 'Who won a jigsaw puzzle in a painting competition in 1956?' (Answer: Me!). Substitute your own achievement! Discuss whether or not all these achievements were of equal worth. 'Why/why not?'

B. Ask: 'What makes something really worthwhile achieving?' (eg personal satisfaction, it will benefit others etc). Point out that complete dedication to a task carries with it the danger of neglecting other important areas (eg family, friends).

C. Try this experiment: Find a large, strong glass jar with a fairly small opening. Place an object inside like a softball which can be squeezed into the jar but not got out. Choose two or three pupils to try to retrieve the ball. Warning: Make sure that the glass jar won't break and no one will get their hand stuck! Show that to get their hand out, they have to let go of the ball, and to achieve something that is really worthwhile, one may have to give up or let go of certain other things (eg two hours of TV to prepare for a test next day, hours of training to make the school team). Use earlier questions to talk about the kind of sacrifices some people have made in order to help others and the intense training and dedication of people like the snooker player Steve Davis.

D. In the 1940s in the Auschwitz prison camp in Germany a Roman Catholic priest, Maximilian Kolbe, went to the gas chambers instead of Franciszek, the father of a Polish family. Kolbe did achieve something important in his own view.[1] Ask: 'Do you think this was worthwhile?' 'What motivated him?'

E. Read the two quotes from Paul.

I am bringing all my energies to bear on this one thing: Forgetting the past and looking forward to what lies ahead, I strain to reach the end of the race and receive the prize for which God is calling us up to heaven because of what Christ Jesus did for us (Philippians 3:13–14).

In a race, everyone runs but only one person gets first prize. So run your race to win. To win the contest you must deny yourselves many things that would keep you from doing your best. An athlete goes to all this trouble just to win a blue ribbon or a silver cup, but we do it for a heavenly reward that never disappears. So I run straight to the goal with purpose in every step. I fight to win. I'm not just shadow-boxing or playing around (1 Corinthians 9:24–27).

Paul believed that God had a particular task for him to do (ie to make the Good News of Jesus' love known to lots of people), and he wanted nothing to get in the way of achieving that goal. He was so sure of this, that he was prepared to face persecution, go to prison, even to die for what he believed in so that he could achieve the 'prize'.

F. Suggest that some people might like to seek God's help in achieving their goals and in getting their priorities right by using the following prayer:

> Lord, show us what is worth achieving in our life. Help us pursue these goals in our lives with courage and determination and help us let go of unimportant little ambitions or pleasures which distract us from the main aim.

## IDEAS FOR DEVELOPMENT

Do a follow-up project on Maximilian Kolbe or Charles T. Studd, a famous cricketer of his day who gave up his successful career to become a missionary in China.[2]

## FOOTNOTES

[1] *Franciszek And Father Maximilian* (Catholic Truth Society: London, 1987), ISBN 0 85183 732 8.

[2] John Godwin, *More Lives To Inspire—Stories For School Assemblies* (Moorley's Publishing: Ilkeston, 1980), ISBN 0 86071 087 4, p 68. Assembly outline on Kolbe.
Kathleen White, *C. T. Studd—Cricketer & Crusader* (Marshall-Pickering: Basingstoke, 1985), ISBN 0 551 01245 5.

# 7

## THEME

# The Bible

**AIM**

To consider the Christian belief that the Bible can still speak powerfully to the modern world.

**INTRODUCTION**

Explain that the pupils of Greenway Boy's Comprehensive School in Bristol were working on a Bible project with their teacher who asked: 'How would you encourage other teenagers to look at the Bible?' In response to this, one boy suggested writing to some famous people to find out which bit of the Bible they liked best. He said: 'If their hero reads the Bible they might look at it.' One result of their enquiries was the book *Best Bible Bits* which contains replies from a number of celebrities. Read the following letters to the group and look up the Bible passages to which these people refer:

BBC Television Centre
Wood Lane
London W12

Dear Richard Lovell,

Thank you for writing to me. My favourite reading from the Bible is Psalm twenty-three. In the sort of work I do I often have moments when I'm very nervous and apprehensive—for instance before making my entrance on a first night. I repeat the Psalm to myself quietly in the dressing room and I'm quite sure I'm given strength to approach my work with a positive attitude, knowing that God is with me to help and support me.

Best wishes to you, the other children, and the teachers at your school.

Yours sincerely,
Wendy Craig.

Dear Richard Long,

My favourite story from the Bible is the parable of the labourers in the vineyard [Matthew 20:1–16], as it is a marvellous lesson about the dissatisfaction that can be caused by Envy—which is, in my opinion, one of the most destructive forces in the world today.

Yours sincerely,
Ronnie Barker.

British Broadcasting Corp.
Lime Grove Studios
London W12 7RJ
Telephone 01-743 8000
Telex 265781

2nd November 1983

Dear Bobby,

My favourite part of the Bible is the Book of Esther—it is a marvellous story, like Cinderella, of an ordinary girl who becomes a princess—it is the first recorded beauty contest, which was won with her intelligence—and obviously I have had to read it quite often myself as I was named after her!

Best wishes.
Yours sincerely,
Esther Rantzen[1]

## OPTIONS AND IDEAS

A. Help pupils to prepare a simple letter to send to some prominent local Christians and church leaders asking them for a favourite Bible 'bit' and the reason for their choice. Set aside another time for sharing the replies.

B. Explain that Christians believe the Bible to be 'the word of God' which, among other things, contains rules for living, promises from God and eyewitness accounts of the life of Jesus. Christians think of the Bible as a 'living book', in that it has the power to communicate with people today about God.

C. Read the following extract from the book *Coming Home* to show how reading from the Bible had a powerful effect on a young man's life. Background notes: Len Magee had a disturbed childhood in London followed by several tough but happy years at an Australian farm school. As a teenager, he became immersed in the

Sydney pop and drugs culture of the Sixties, eventually returning to England via the 'hippy-trail' in a desperate search to find his mother and satisfy a growing hunger for contentment and meaning in life. Having not seen his mother for fourteen years, their eventual meeting was traumatic. Then one night something happened which was to change Len's life. This is how he describes it:

> I was rummaging about on top of the wardrobe when I unearthed an old Bible. It was my father's— it had his name in it—and out of curiosity I began flicking through it. Strangely, I felt myself drawn to it, as though I had an appetite to read.
>
> Suddenly a picture flashed up on my memory and I remembered a time when I was in Sydney and a guy said to me, 'Hey, man, you wanna try reading the Bible on LSD. It's a real trip!' Well, I had no LSD, but I could get pretty high on opium so I thought maybe I would try that, perhaps tomorrow.... Even so, I couldn't deny this extraordinary desire to read and so I sat on the edge of the bed and flicked through, reading a few verses here and there at random. I don't recall what I read, but I do know that it did something for me—gave me a good feeling—and the appetite grew. Oddly, the Bible no longer seemed a dead book, dry and boring and meaningless; somehow it seemed to be coming to life. And although I didn't realise it at the time, God was beginning to operate in my life.... That night I returned home with a real hunger to read more. First things first, though, and after dinner I went off down the shed for a joint. I wasn't particularly interested in the idea of reading the Bible while on a trip—I was just feeding the habit; besides, what I'd read the previous night seemed to be a sort of trip in itself—and when I got upstairs and took the

book in my hands again it was with a certain amount of excitement...the thrill of discovery!...As I read on and on, verse after verse, chapter after chapter, I began to learn how God dealt with men, and again I was struck by the wonder of it all, the awefulness...and slowly, very slowly, I began to see myself in relation to God's greatness: small, insignificant, worthless, wretched.... For the first time I was seeing myself as I really was, as though God was peeling back the surface of my life to reveal the rottenness within.[2]

D. Allow opportunity for pupils to read Psalm 119:96–105 which illustrates the importance of God's 'word'—the Bible—to believers.

## IDEAS FOR DEVELOPMENT

Hire the video or soundstrip *How To Beat The System*.[3]

## FOOTNOTES

[1] Janet Green, *Best Bible Bits* (CIO Publishing: London, 1984), ISBN 0 7151 0420 9, pp 21-23, 57-58.

[2] Abridged from: Len Magee/Chris Spencer, *Coming Home—The Len Magee Story* (Lakeland/Marshall Morgan & Scott: London, 1980), ISBN 0 551 00864 4, pp 149-151.

[3] *How To Beat The System* (Scripture Union, 130 City Road, London EC1V 2NJ, 1979). This is a twelve-minute humorous cartoon about Sidney Penge's head, the Head Monitor, which begins to panic when Sidney considers buying and reading a Bible. (Available in video or soundstrip format.)

# 8

## THEME
# Consequences

**AIM**
   i) To think about the effects of irresponsible or anti-social behaviour.
   ii) To help pupils understand Christian teaching about responsibility to God.

**INTRODUCTION**
Initiate a brief game of 'Consequences'. For this game everyone needs a piece of paper which is to be passed on to the next six persons in a round. The first person writes down a name (Who?), folds it and passes it on to the next person who writes a verb/action (Did What?). The third player puts down 'With' and another name (With Whom?). The fourth writes down a place (Where?), the fifth a time or date (When?). The sixth makes up what could happen as a result (and the consequences were....). Read out some of the resulting sentences.

## OPTIONS AND IDEAS

A. Talk about the pride many people felt about England's football team performance in the 1990 Football World Cup, as well as the good behaviour of the fans. Contrast this with serious incidents of poor behaviour by fans and the consequences of their actions (eg events at Heysel—one reason for the ban on English clubs competing in European competitions).

B. Draw up a chart to indicate possible consequences of irresponsible behaviour:

| | |
|---|---|
| Not doing homework ................ | .................. |
| Neglecting your health .............. | .................. |
| Spreading hurtful rumours .......... | .................. |
| Disregarding instructions ........... | .................. |
| Being jealous or spiteful ............ | .................. |
| Living only for the present moment | .................. |

C. The Bible teaches that people are accountable to God, the ruler of the universe, and that he holds human beings responsible for their actions. Look up and read Galatians 6:7–9. Christians believe that left to our own devices everybody would earn condemnation, but that those who bring their failures to God will be forgiven and receive life instead of death. The Bible shows that God can turn failures around so that they can produce a positive outcome.

D. Look at the information below about some characters from the Bible. Ask: 'How would you rate their actions?' 'Are the consequences or resulting situations positive or negative?':

*Joseph* tells his dreams to his family. His brothers are jealous and sell him as a slave to Egypt. After having started a career as an administrator/manager he is sent to prison for a few years due to no fault of his own. Because he can interpret Pharaoh's dreams he is promoted to become the governor of the whole country. Through this post he is able to help save his family (his father and his brothers) from starvation and be reconciled with his brothers (retold from Genesis 37—45).

*Jacob* bribes his brother into giving him his rights as the first-born son and then deceives his father. When the whole affair is found out, he runs away to escape his brother's anger. On his way to his uncle Laban he has a dream which makes him commit his life to God in the hope that God will look after him. At Laban's he is made to work seven years for Rachel (Laban's daughter)—the girl he loves. On the wedding day he is cheated by Laban and gets Leah as his wife and not Rachel. Laban lets Jacob have Rachel as well for another seven years of labour for him. After another bargain with Laban, Jacob flees from him into his home country. There he is anxious about meeting his brother Esau but in the end he is reconciled with him (retold from Genesis 25—33).

Jesus and his disciples are out in an olive grove at night. Some chief priests and Pharisees approach wanting to arrest Jesus who is identified by Judas. *Peter* is quick to draw his sword out and cut off the ear of the High Priest's slave. After Jesus is arrested, his courage fails even though he follows Jesus into the courtyard of the High Priest's house. Here three times he denies knowing Jesus, but is sorry for it afterwards. When Jesus reappears after his resurrection he has a special conversation with Peter in which he reassures Peter and gives him an important role to play in the church (retold from John 18—21).

## IDEAS FOR DEVELOPMENT

Collect together some current stories from the news which illustrate the suffering caused in the world by people's greed or irresponsible behaviour.

Devise your own sequence of consequences, based on one of the Bible stories. Choose one of the Biblical characters above (eg Peter), and describe the original action, ie cutting one soldier's ear off. Imagine two possible consequences for him—(A) he is arrested with Jesus or (B) Jesus doesn't heal the ear as in the biblical story. Imagine what the consequences could have been, ie if Peter had been arrested with Jesus he could have been beaten up badly (A.1) or if Jesus had not healed the soldier's ear he could have run away with the other disciples—out of fear that they would be arrested as well (B.1). The following structure might help:

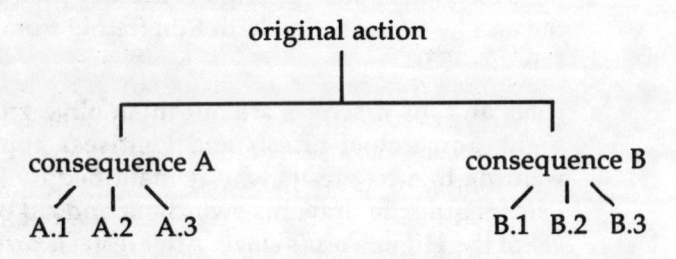

```
                original action
        ┌──────────────┴──────────────┐
   consequence A                 consequence B
    ╱   │   ╲                     ╱   │   ╲
   A.1 A.2 A.3                   B.1 B.2 B.3
```

# 9

## THEME
# Worry

**AIM**
  i) To show pupils the negative effect of worry.
  ii) To consider the positive effects of trusting in God.

**INTRODUCTION**
Read the poem 'Whatif':

> Last night, while I lay thinking here,
> Some Whatifs crawled inside my ear
> And pranced and partied all night long
> And sang their same old Whatif song:
> Whatif I'm dumb in school?
> Whatif they've closed the swimming pool?
> Whatif I get beat up?
> Whatif there's poison in my cup?
> Whatif I start to cry?
> Whatif I get sick and die?
> Whatif I flunk that test?
> Whatif green hair grows on my chest?
> Whatif nobody likes me?

Whatif a bolt of lightning strikes me?
Whatif I don't grow taller?
Whatif my head starts getting smaller?
Whatif the fish won't bite?
Whatif the wind tears up my kite?
Whatif they start a war?
Whatif my parents get divorced?
Whatif the bus is late?
Whatif my teeth don't grow in straight?
Whatif I tear my pants?
Whatif I never learn to dance?
Everything seems swell, and then
The nighttime Whatifs strike again![1]

Afterwards ask: 'What are the "Whatifs" that worry you?' 'How often have you worried about something that didn't actually happen?'

## OPTIONS AND IDEAS

A. Pick up on the poem by saying that we often worry about the future and we think about all the possible things that could go wrong. Discuss the type of things people worry about. Suggest that most people worry about starting something new like a new job, a new school, etc. Look at the following prayer:

Dear God, I'm scared.
I've seen the big school.
We went last term to look round.
But you know what it's like, anyway.
There are big boys there.
We were the biggest in our school.
It's going to feel strange.
The teachers aren't like ours.
We'll be having lots of them.
We have to go to different rooms
all round the school.

I'm frightened I'll get lost.
There's corridors all over the place, Lord.
I suppose you know all about that too.
Help me to find somebody to show me the ropes.
Please let me feel like I belong
to this new school.
After all, it's my school now.[2]

Ask if anyone remembers feeling rather like this when they changed schools.

B. Some people are so anxious to know what the future holds for them that they read their horoscopes regularly, or even visit a fortune teller in an attempt to find out. Christians believe that this is not a wise way of dealing with worry and can be harmful. They believe that their future is secure in God's hands because God has proved himself to be dependable in the past. This means he is in control of all that happens now and everything that will happen in the future, as indicated in Matthew 6:25-34. Give pupils the opportunity for quiet reflecting on personal worries which some may like to incorporate into a prayer requesting God's help. (Refer back to the prayer above for ideas on how to write this.)

C. Learn the sketch 'Do Not Worry' which can involve one or two narrators and the class responding to them through actions (as indicated in brackets). Perform it as a whole class in another year's class assembly or in the hall. It is based on Matthew 6:25-34.

Narrator(s):

And gathering the crowds to Him,
(All bunch together, excited)
He said—You *could* worry about tomorrow;
(Bite nails, tremble)

There might be an earthquake,
(All stagger)
An epidemic of fleas,
(Scratch)
Or a cash crisis.
(Turn out pockets, pass hat round)
You could lose your job,
(Look bored)
Your home,
(Look round)
Or your marbles!
(Act crazy)
You might fall in love,
(Hand on heart, pout lips)
Catch mumps,
(Cheeks and eyes bulge)
Or fall in love *and* catch mumps!
(Heart, pout lips, cheeks bulge)
It may be your birthday,
(Sing 'Happy Birthday', blow out candles)
Or Christmas,
(Carols, crackers, etc)
Or Guy Fawkes.
(Fireworks)
It may be your anniversary—
(Boys look surprised)
and you *may* forget!
(Girls look angry)
FREEZE
But what's the point?
(All shrug)
On the other hand—
(All look at hand)
You could concentrate on today,
(All think hard)
And God's love.
(Look up surprised)

After all, do the flowers follow fashions?
(Girls look glamorous/boys pick flowers)
Do the birds work shifts?
(Flap wings and tweet)
Does the grass take out an insurance policy?
(One mows lawn loudly and runs over another's foot)
And yet God looks after them.
(Different poses of protecting)
So do not worry about tomorrow,
(Bite nails)
Your Father knows what you need.
(Look up surprised)
Instead—be concerned about the Kingdom of God and what He requires of you,
(Point to audience)
And He'll take care of the rest.
(Freeze looking up)[3]

## IDEAS FOR DEVELOPMENT

See how God provided for the Hebrews during their escape out of Egypt and their journey through the desert, by studying highlights of their early history.[4]

Arrange to fit in some pastoral input on strategies for work and taking exams.

**FOOTNOTES**

[1] Shel Silverstein, 'Whatif' in: Patricia McCall/Sue Palmer, *Presenting Poetry 2* (Oliver & Boyd: Edinburgh, 1986), ISBN 0 05 003726 9, p 14. Originally from: Shel Silverstein, *A Light In The Attic* (Jonathan Cape).

[2] Janet Green, *Home-made Prayers* (Lion Publishing: Tring, 1983), ISBN 0 85848 211 0, p 10.

[3] 'Do Not Worry' in: Dave Hopwood, *Acting On Impulse* (Lee Abbey: Lynton, 1987), p 12.

[4] Linda Smith, *All About Living 2* (Lion Publishing: Tring, 1986), ISBN 0 7459 1161 7, pp 2-38.
Andrew Goldstein, *Exploring The Bible—Founders To Judges* (Religious and Moral Education Press: Exeter, 1987), ISBN 0 08 035111 5, pp 25-38.
Gerald Hughes/Stephen Travis, *The Birth Of A Nation* (Lion Publishing: Tring, 1981), ISBN 0 85648 263 3, pp 13-21.
Sue Phillips, *Moses and Other Stories* (Longman: Harlow, 1988), ISBN 0 582 31116 0, pp 19-29.
C. M. Amos, *Israel Becomes A Nation* (Hulton Educational Publications: Amersham, 1984), ISBN 0 7175 1160 X, pp 26-41.

# 10

## THEME

# Be Yourself

**AIM**
  i) To help pupils to accept themselves as they really are.
  ii) To consider the Christian belief that God is willing to receive anyone into his family.

**INTRODUCTION**
Use an acorn and a few different packets of seeds to illustrate the variety of trees, flowers and vegetables that can be grown.

**OPTIONS AND IDEAS**

A. Continue with the acorn/seed illustration by pointing out that it would be amazing if they planted cabbage seeds and sweet peas came up; or if they planted an acorn and an apple tree was the result. Show them the importance of accepting themselves as they are and being able to identify the positive aspects of their character and personality and talents.

B. Prepare two pupils to perform the sketch 'The Parable Of The Fruit Trees':

1. (Unimpressed, looking at 2 sideways) Oranges again, eh?
2. (Who's been admiring the view) Hmm...what?
1. I see you've got oranges again.
2. (Excitedly) Yes, two weeks early this year.
1. I'm surprised you don't get bored growing them things.
2. (Cheerfully) Oh, no!
1. I know I'd get bored growing oranges all the time.
2. Just as well you're an apple tree then, isn't it? (Pause)
1. I get bored with apples as well.
2. Oh dear, not exactly your day, is it?
1. All those pips in your roots.
2. Could be worse—you could be stuck with melons.
1. (With a withering look at 2) Melons don't grow on trees.
2. Lucky for you then, isn't it?
1. Anyway, I've had enough of apples. That's why I'm changing my fruit this year.
2. What?
1. Figs.
2. Figs?
1. Figs. I'm gonna grow figs. I rather like the shape myself.
2. Oh no you're not.
1. Yes I am.
2. You are not.
1. I am.
2. You are *not*.
1. Why not?

2. Because you can't, you're an apple tree. That's why not.
1. I *was* an apple tree. But now (Folds arm) I'm gonna be a fig tree.
2. You're mad.
1. And next year, I may even be a grape vine—I haven't decided yet.
2. Well, what's the gardener going to say about that?
1. Nothing. It's my decision.
2. But he planted you. He looks after you.
1. Well, he doesn't have to anymore, I'll do it myself.
2. Oh yes? And just where are you going to get the water from?
1. (Stumped)...I'll er...I'll pray for a wet summer.
2. (Looking up) Yes, well, I have to admit—you'll be all right on that one. But this is so silly.
1. There's nothing more to be said. From now on (Holds arm out) I'm a fig tree. (An apple drops from 1's hand)
2. Then what's this? A fig with an identity crisis?
1. Where did that come from?
2. You! Because you're an apple tree. Whatever you might think... *this* is the fruit you were made for. (Both freeze)[1]

Discuss the meaning behind this parable and the danger of sometimes wanting to be something we are not.

C. Give each pupil a slip of paper. Ask them to write down their responses to the following questions: (a) 'What quality do you most like about yourself?' (b) 'Which of your character traits are you not happy about?' (c) 'What would make you happier with yourself or your situation?' If appropriate, give time to talk about some of their answers. (This may need sensitive handling.)

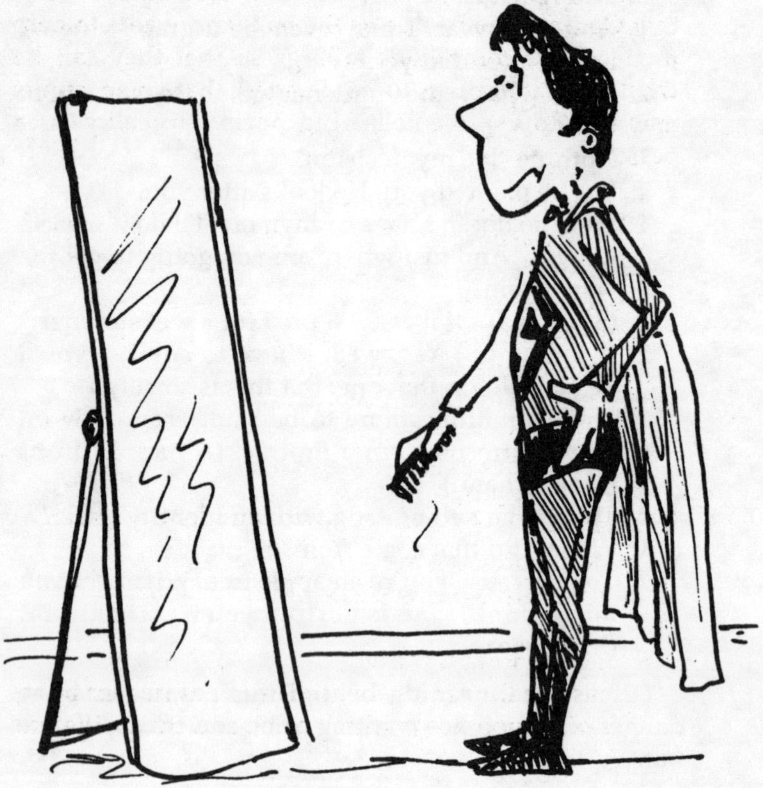

D. Provoke discussion on the idea that striving to be 'Superman' or 'Superwoman' might be a symptom of insecurity with what we are. Ask: 'Is this the case?' 'Do we present the world with a false picture of ourselves?' 'If so, why?' Explain that Christians believe that God accepts people as they are and wants to help them to overcome their failings so that they can be what he wants them to be. Suggest that some pupils may like to use the following poem 'Unreality' as a personal prayer:

> In this mechanical world of
> false eyelashes,
> false teeth,
> contact lenses,
> fantastic face lifts,
> eye-deceiving hair pieces
> and surgically removed bulges—
> please help me to become
> what eternity planned me to be.
> For I suspect that striving to be
> what I am not
> is little more than symptoms
> of insecurity with what I am.[2]

## IDEAS FOR DEVELOPMENT

Find out the variety of seeds such as runner bean, pea or onion seeds which exist, and their different characteristics.

**FOOTNOTES**

[1] 'The Parable Of The Fruit Trees' in: Dave Hopwood, *Acting On Impulse* (Lee Abbey: Lynton, 1987), pp 5-6.
[2] 'Unreality' in: Phil Streeter, *The Divinity Of Daydreams* (1986).

## 11

**THEME**

# The Disaster Movie

**AIM**
- i) To reflect on the role of authority in our lives.
- ii) To help pupils to understand that God is a legitimate authority.

**INTRODUCTION**

Talk about disaster movies pupils may have seen on TV such as *The Towering Inferno*, *Hotel* or more recently the take offs of these films in *Airplane I* and *II*. When these films first started they were very exciting and drew large audiences. Now they are less popular because so many of them have been made. They seem to be written to a formula, and to share many common ingredients. Ask the students to volunteer their own suggestions for the ingredients of a disaster movie. If they're short of ideas use the 'recipe' below:

1) A large hotel, ship, plane, bridge, skyscraper or any sizable structure that can take a large

number of people and have a potential for disaster.
2) A mixed group of passengers. You must include a sick child, and if possible, a singing nun!
3) A budding romance.
4) A disaster. A fatal flaw in the structure, a fire, a bomb, an accident just waiting to happen.
5) To set the scene you need a few clues laid early in the film, a glimpse of smoking wiring, a weather report warning of tornadoes, a warning from the architect or chief fire officer which is ignored. This is a vital element as they need to be able to say 'I told you so' later on in the film.
6) You need the hero/heroine. If possible, make this the person who tried to warn them early on, then they can be really smug.

## OPTIONS AND IDEAS

A. Read the outline of the disaster movie plot below. Warn pupils that they have to write an ending to the story.

> The pilot of a Concorde has just had a heart attack and is unconscious, the co-pilot is writhing in agony with food poisoning. The auto pilot has broken down. There are desperately ill people on board. The steward asks if anyone can fly a plane. One lady volunteers, she has had a few lessons in a light aircraft but has never flown 'solo'! She walks into the cockpit and nearly faints when she sees the terrifying array of instruments...[1]

B. Invite a few pupils to read out their conclusions to the movie plot. Comment that in these films the plane is usually saved by being put under the direction of the control tower. Someone who knows what they were doing needs to manage the plane or it is left hurtling through the air in grave danger. Christians sometimes feel people are a little like a plane in a disaster movie. The pilot (God) is no longer in control because people have rejected him. Ask: 'Where do people look for guidance on how to live if the pilot is out of action?' Some people turn to fortune tellers, reading horoscopes or rely on the advice of friends. Point out that Christians ask God to be in control of their lives.

C. Think about some occasions when it would be very necessary to follow instructions and to do exactly as one is told, without questioning it (eg in a fire, in a driving test, etc). Ask: 'What might happen if people did not do as instructed?'

D. Authority is the right to exercise power. Make a list of people or groups who exercise power and authority over you. Look at each one in turn and decide what your response should be to them. Get pupils to give examples of times when it might be right to disobey people in authority. Make a second list to show over whom you exercise some authority (eg a younger brother or sister).

E. Read the account of the exchange between Jesus and Pontius Pilate at Jesus' trial:

> He [Pilate] took Jesus into the palace again and asked him, 'Where are you from?', but Jesus gave no answer. 'You won't talk to me?' Pilate demanded. 'Don't you realise I have the power to release you or to crucify you?' Then Jesus said, 'You would have no power at all over me unless it were given to you from above. So those who brought me to you have the greater sin' (John 19:9–11).

Point especially to Jesus' reply to Pilate which indicates that Pilate could only exercise power and authority as God allowed. Christians believe that God's power and authority is to be submitted to willingly because God loves them and has their interests at heart. A prime example of this principle was Jesus himself. He submitted to the will of God and even allowed himself to be crucified.

## IDEAS FOR DEVELOPMENT

Look up some past and present examples of people who have disobeyed people in authority because of personal or religious convictions (eg Polycarp, the Bishop of Smyrna, who, at eighty-six years of age, was seized by the Romans, and because he would not deny his faith, was sent to his death in the arena).[2] Examples from present times are the Russian Pastor Georgi Vins or Rumanian Pastor Richard Wurmbrand who were both arrested under Communist regimes for spreading Christianity.[3]

## FOOTNOTES

[1] This originally appeared in: Margaret Cooling, *War and Pacifism* (Scripture Union: London, 1988), ISBN 0 86201 389 5, p 45.
[2] 'St Polycarp' in: Charles Moreton, *Time To Grow—Book 1* (Angel Press: Chichester, 1985), ISBN 0 947785 01 9, p 28.
[3] 'Georgi Vins' in: John Godwin, *More Lives To Inspire* (Moorley's Publishing: Ilkeston, 1980), ISBN 0 86071 087 4, pp 96-97.
Mary Drewery, *Richard Wurmbrand—The Man Who Came Back* (Marshall Pickering: Basingstoke, 1983), ISBN 0 551 01039 8.
Elizabeth Hicks, *Living Dangerously—Stories Of Brave Christians* (Scripture Union: London, 1986), ISBN 0 86201 355 0, pp 83-95.

# 12

### THEME
# Selfishness

**AIM**

To demonstrate some of the negative aspects of selfish behaviour and some positive results of self-lessness.

**INTRODUCTION**

Present a dart board or a target and some darts or a bow and arrow. Invite some pupils to try and hit the goal: the bullseye or target, either with a dart or an arrow.

**OPTIONS AND IDEAS:**

A. Explain that Christians might compare peoples' lives with an arrow or dart which misses the mark. The Bible talks about people being imperfect and 'missing the mark' or 'deviating from the goal' which God has set. Christians believe that Jesus, on the contrary, lived a perfect life without selfishness and that 'his arrow went straight into the target.'

B. Read the story 'The Unselfish Gift':

A wicked woman died. As her punishment she was condemned to eternal torment. In her agony she cried out for mercy. At length an angel answered, 'I can help you if you can remember one altogether unselfish thing you did while on earth'. It seemed easy, but when she began to recite her good deeds, she realised that every one of them had been done from a motive of self-interest. Finally, at the point of despair, she remembered a carrot she had once given to a beggar. She feared to mention it, because it had been a poor, withered carrot that she would never have used in the stew she was preparing. But the angel consulted the record, and the record showed that the act had been promoted by unselfishness, not great unselfishness or it would have been a better gift, but unselfishness none the less. So down the limitless space that separates Heaven from Hell the carrot was lowered on a slender string. Could this weak thing bear her weight and lift her out of torment? It did not seem possible, but desperation made her try. She grasped the withered carrot and slowly began to rise. Then she felt a weight dragging her. She looked down and saw other tormented souls clinging to her, hoping to escape with her. 'Let go, let go,' she cried. 'The carrot won't hold us all.' But grimly, desperately, they held on. Again she cried, 'Let go, let go! This is MY carrot!' At that point the string broke, and, still clutching the carrot she had reclaimed for herself the woman fell back into the pains of Hell. This sums up the fate of anyone who lives by the philosophy 'What's mine, is mine!' In the long run, he gets the carrot—nothing more![1]

Ask pupils for their reaction to this. Suggest they might spend a moment or two quietly thinking about times when they have been selfish as well as occasions when they have offered help to others in some way.

C. Refer to the story of *The Lion, The Witch And The Wardrobe* by reading some extracts or by showing a clip from either the BBC production or the comic strip version.[2] Draw up a list of ways in which Edmund was selfish and the results of his selfishness (eg he gave the witch a lot of information that he shouldn't have given her just in order to get sweets; he felt sick after eating so many turkish delights; he denied having been to Narnia and upset Lucy; he betrayed his brother and his sisters and put their lives in danger).

D. Look up the story of the 'Lost Son', also called the Prodigal Son, in Luke 15:11–32. Discuss the effects of his selfishness on his father, brother and the rest of the household.

E. Some pupils may like to use the following prayer:

> Forgive me, Lord, for the times when I have thought only about myself, and others have suffered in some way. (Pause to give pupils time to think about this). Please help me to put other people and their interests first so that we may all live and work together as you would want us to.

**IDEAS FOR DEVELOPMENT**

Challenge pupils to think of one particular thing they could do for someone else in the coming week and do it. Arrange a 'report back' session.

**FOOTNOTES**

[1] A. Leonard Griffith, 'The Unselfish Gift' in: John Bailey (ed), *Blueprint Book Four* (Galliard/Stainer & Bell: London 1976), ISBN 0 85249 354 1, p 1063. Originally from: A. Leonard Griffith: *What Is A Christian?* (Hodder & Stoughton).

[2] C. S. Lewis, *The Lion, The Witch And The Wardrobe* (Fontana Lions/Collins: London, 1950 reprinted 1980), pp 36-43.
C. S. Lewis, *The Chronicles Of Narnia—The Lion, The Witch And The Wardrobe* (BBC Enterprises Ltd: London, 1990). A BBC TV production in video format, available from some local video shops.
C. S. Lewis, *The Lion, The Witch And The Wardrobe* (Vestron Video International/Children's Video Library, London, 1985). Animated cartoon video. Duration: ninety-five minutes.

# 13

## THEME
# The Power Of Attraction

**AIM**
> To explore the drawing power and magnetism of some people and places.

**INTRODUCTION**
> Show a powerful magnet or magnetically operated toy. A compass would also be useful as a visual aid.

**OPTIONS AND IDEAS**

A. Try out which materials are attracted by a magnet (things made of steel, iron or nickel). Explain how the word 'magnetism' is taken from an ancient city called Magnesia where many lodestones (ie natural magnets) were found. The lodestone is a magnetic rock which, when suspended on a cord always points to the north. This is why it was used as a compass.

B. Talk about various 'magnetic' personalities and the way in which people are drawn to such persons. Have some pictures to show of famous people who attract large followings. Ask pupils to contribute further examples.

C. Ask: 'What draws us to certain people?' and 'What sort of effect can such people have on us?' (eg why we want to be with these people or why we may want to copy the way they dress or behave, etc).

D. Put pupils into groups and give them the task of inventing a 'Super Hero' who has the power to attract large numbers of people and builds up a very large following. Ask them to list their hero's main qualities or abilities which give them such appeal. Ensure there will be a spokesperson capable of relaying the finished result.

E. Christians would not regard Jesus simply as a 'Super Hero' but God in human form. According to the Gospel records Jesus attracted crowds of people to himself. Illustrate this point with examples:

| Who? | Why? | Where? |
| --- | --- | --- |
| A crowd | Jesus explained to them in simple words and with authority what God is like and how people should treat each other. | Matthew 5-7 |
| A blind man Bartimaeus | Jesus healed him. | Mark 10:46-52 |
| A crowd | Jesus fed a great crowd with a small amount of food. | Matthew 15:29-38 |
| Zacchaeus | Jesus loved outsiders and spent time with them. | Luke 19:1-10 |

| Woman at the well | He treated women with respect in a society in which women were seen as the property of their husbands. | John 4:1-26 |
| A Roman soldier | He realised after Jesus' death that Jesus spoke the truth about himself and was the Son of God. | Luke 23:47 |

F. Point out that nearly 2000 years after the death of Jesus, people all over the world claim to be followers of the Christian faith including some well-known personalities. For example, in 1986 Glenn Hoddle was part of the England squad for the FA World Cup finals which were to take place in Mexico later in the year. Israel was chosen as a basis for the pre-World Cup preparation. Journeying to the Middle East the team was taken to Jerusalem and Bethlehem. Read about the impression this had on him or watch the relevant clip from the video.

> Glenn was absolutely thrilled by what he saw. He had always seen Jesus as an important historical figure in a much told story, but no more than that. Now Jesus began to emerge as a highly relevant person for life in the present, especially for *his* life.[1]

Ask pupils to suggest what attracts people to the Christian faith.

G. Read the following prayer in a meditative style. It was written by some Christians for a celebration service.

> You're ace, Lord.
> You're bigger than me and all my fears.
> You hold my hand and make me look at those things
> That terrify me.
> When I look, they are gone.

>    They cannot stand before you.
>    You're ace, Lord.
>    You're the best.[2]

H.  Think about some famous places that attract pilgrims and tourists from all over the world (eg Lourdes, Israel, Mecca, Taizé, Spring Harvest, Greenbelt, etc).[3] Ask for further examples to add to the list. Working in pairs, ask pupils to suggest what attracts people to each of these places.

## IDEAS FOR DEVELOPMENT

Collect pictures of places or people that attract others.

Make a magnet by striking a needle with a magnet. Try to magnetise other objects (ie a screwdriver, penknife or a pair of scissors, etc). What objects can be magnetised?

Show some slides about Taizé, a place which attracts people from all over the world.[4]

## FOOTNOTES

[1] Tony Jasper (ed), *Moments Of Truth* (Marshall Pickering: London, 1990), ISBN 0 551 01876 3, p 60.
*Hoddle* (International Films, The Coach House, 55 Drayton Green, London W13 0JD). Video portrait of the soccer star Glenn Hoddle. Duration: forty minutes.

[2] From the service sheet of the final celebration service at the Creative Arts Conference at Lee Abbey in October 1990.

[3] Spring Harvest (14 Horsted Square, Uckfield, East Sussex TN22 1QL) is a national week-long gathering of Christians at different sites such as Minehead, Skegness, Ayr. It is usually around Easter. Greenbelt Festival (The Greenhouse, St Luke's Church, Hillmarton Road, London N7 9JE) is an annual Christian Arts festival in Northamptonshire, usually over August Bank Holiday.

[4] *Taizé* (Mowbray: Oxford, 1984), ISBN 0 264 67009 4. Cassette and slide set.
*Taizé—Trust Is At Hand* (A & PT: Taizé, 1989). This video is available from Cassell plc, Stanley House, 3 Fleets Lane, Poole, Dorset BH15 3AJ.

# 14
## THEME
# Dreams And Schemes

**AIM**

To challenge pupils to think about their own potential and how it might be realised.

**INTRODUCTION**

Select six pupils and ask the rest of the group which of them might become (a) a nurse, (b) an engineer, (c) a building society manager, (d) a teacher, (e) a famous football player, (f) a brain surgeon, (g) a pop star. Point out that it is not possible to work out what everyone will become but each one might have certain aims in life—dreams of what they want to become.

**OPTIONS AND IDEAS**

A. Most pupils will know the story of the 'Ugly Duckling'.[1] Refer to the story to illustrate the point that we don't always see our own potential. The duckling wanted to be beautiful—and potentially he was! Point out that sometimes other people may see our potential when we don't. Ask pupils if their parents or grandparents have dreams for them about what they might be one day. Let them share some of these. What do they think about these ideas?

B. Get some pupils to share some of the dreams they have had. Ask them if any of them have ever come true. Discuss the following statements:

1) All success begins with a dream.
2) There are no great men: only great ideas.
3) You can often measure the size of a man by the size of his dreams.
4) If you don't have a dream, how can dreams come true?[2]

C. Ask pupils: 'What do you really want out of life?' Tell them: 'Now think hard how you could achieve it'. Make some suggestions like: working hard, visiting the Careers Office, practising, etc. Get pupils to devise their own personal goals' chart. Suggest they use the headings: activity/interest, weekly goal, monthly goal, by next year. Help them to set themselves some realistic targets for school work, leisure activities, personal pursuits, etc.

D. Relate this fictional conversation of Jesus'. Jesus knew the potential that his disciples had, and that they achieved it by trusting in God's help.

The story is told about a conversation Jesus had with an angel, shortly after Jesus' ascension to heaven. The angel asked him, 'What plans have you made to ensure that your work of extending the kingdom will continue now that you've returned to heaven?' Jesus replied that he had commissioned twelve men to carry on his mission on earth. 'And what if they fail?' asked the angel. 'I have no other plans,' replied Jesus. One of the wonderful things about him was that he saw people's potential, trained them, commissioned them and trusted them with a task. Sometimes they proved themselves worthy of his trust and sometimes they failed him. But he trusted them anyway.[3]

E. Tell or read the folk tale about the three trees.[4] Point out that the trees' dreams didn't come true the way they thought and expected they would. That is sometimes true of our own dreams. Christians believe that God has a good plan for their lives and for their future: 'For I know the plans I have for you,' says the Lord. 'They are plans good and not evil, to give you a future and a hope' (Jeremiah 29:11). Invite pupils to think about the significance of this verse of Scripture with a moment of quiet reflection. A piece of background music might be played to create a suitable atmosphere.[5]

F. Some people have great dreams and ambitions whereas other people don't seem to have any plans for their future. Read the poem 'Someone Special' written by a Christian who expresses what many pupils might feel:

> I've always found it hard to imagine
> how my life could have any particular significance
> in the general scheme of things.
> For when I compare myself with other people,
> I'm so depressingly average,
> without anything—that's not embarrassing—
> to make me stand out from the crowd.
> In fact I have quite often felt
> like that girl Lara in the Russian novel
> who, when dead, became
> 'A nameless number, on a list that was later mislaid'.
> But today all that has changed,

because today I discovered
that God loves us as we are
without waiting until we do great things
and become someone that everyone wants to know.
But though he loves us as we are,
he doesn't leave us as we are.
Instead he teaches and trains us
so that we are equipped
to do the things that he has planned
for us to do.
Which, if I can find the way he works it out in practice,
will make my life quite an adventure.[6]

## IDEAS FOR DEVELOPMENT

Make a survey asking adults if they are doing now what they dreamt about when they were young. If so, ask how they have achieved it. If not, ask if they could give any advice on how to fulfil one's dreams based on their own experiences.

## FOOTNOTES

[1] 'The Ugly Duckling' in: Hans Andersen/M. R. James, *Favourite Tales Of Hans Andersen* (Faber & Faber: London, 1978), pp 157-165.

[2] Robert H. Schuller, *Move Ahead With Possibility Thinking* (Fleming H. Revell Company: Old Tappan/New Jersey, 1967), p 188.

[3] 'Jesus Enters Heaven' in: Terry Clutterham (ed), *Alive To God* July 13th 1988 (Scripture Union: London, 1988).

[4] K. D. Harvey, 'Three Trees' in: Tony Jasper (ed), *New Stories For The Junior Assembly* (Blandford Press: Poole, 1983), ISBN 0 7137 1313 5, pp 75-76.
Angela Elwell Hunt/Tim Jonke, *The Tale Of Three Trees—A Traditional Folktale* (Lion Publishing: Oxford, 1989), ISBN 0 7459 1743 7.

[5] 'The Journey Continues' on tape: *Experience Rest Instrumental* (Integrity Music/Word UK: Milton Keynes, 1989). Cassette tape available from most Christian bookshops.

[6] 'Someone Special' in: Marion Stroud, *Just For You* (Lion Publishing: Tring, 1986), ISBN 0 85648 910 7, p 71.

## 15

### THEME
# Jigsaw

**AIM**

To provoke thought about different areas of human life which together, make life complete.

**INTRODUCTION**

Enlarge and photocopy the jigsaw and cut up enough for one between two. Put pupils into pairs and give them the prepared jigsaw. Give a small prize or incentive for the first pair to complete it.

**OPTIONS AND IDEAS**

A. Ask pupils to pick out from the puzzle the three pieces that represent the most important areas of their life (eg being happy, doing what I want, talking to God, etc). See which pieces are most widely chosen. Discuss their choices. Then continue with the following: (a) Suggest that some pieces of the puzzle are particularly important to a committed Christian although other people may not consider them to be relevant. 'Which ones?' 'Why?' (b) 'Which pieces would you associate

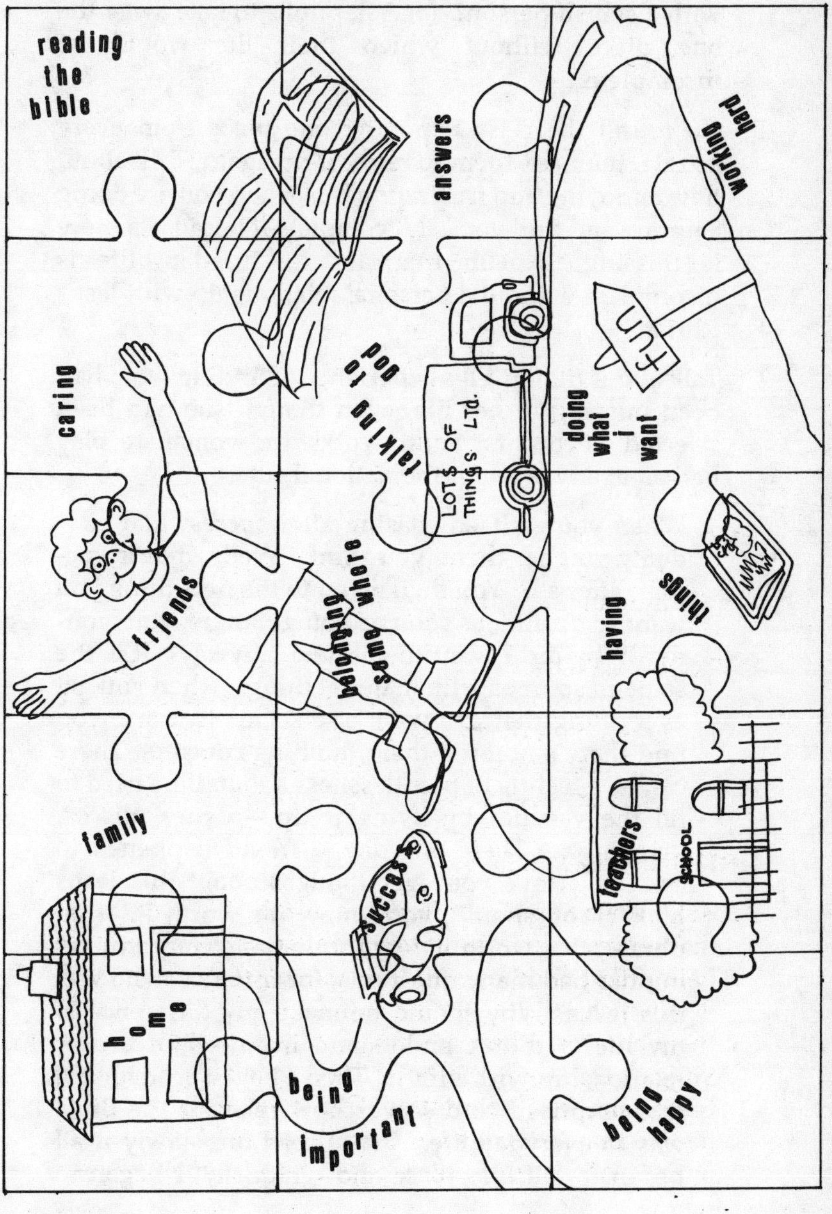

reading the bible
caring
friends
family
home
answers
talking to god
belonging some where
success
being important
working hard
fun
doing what i want
LOTS OF THINGS LTD.
having things
teachers
SCHOOL
being happy

with a selfish person?' (c) Ask pupils to take away the one piece without which their life would be incomplete.

B. Go round the class removing one piece from every puzzle, then ask them to make it up again. Talk about how annoying and frustrating it is when you are doing a jigsaw and find you can't complete it because a piece is missing. Explain that, for a Christian, life is incomplete without a personal relationship with Jesus Christ.

C. Talk about Jill Powell's experience of finding what had been missing in her life, even though she had been selected as the first South Yorkshire woman to play netball at any level for the national side:[1]

> When you've been chasing after success and suddenly you get there, you think, 'Well, what is success, after all?' You then go on to the next thing you want to do and, as soon as you get there, you wonder 'Why did I want to get here, anyway?' It is the same in sport as with material things, when you get everything that everyone else seems to want, you find there's nothing there, nothing concrete. There can be a feeling of pointlessness about life. I tried to fill the vacuum by living it up—parties, discos, drinking.... Then, one day, a friend happened to ask me, 'Have you ever thought about this Jesus bloke? You should, you know, it's worth it.' That phrase, 'It's worth it' went round and round in my mind. I had many questions; for instance, who was this Jesus? Why should he make any difference to my life? I didn't understand my need of a new relationship with him.... Then I began searching. I was surprised to discover how relevant the Bible was to everyday life.... As I read on, slowly it all began to fall into place and, gradually, I began to

change. I felt different inside—I no longer felt that life was pointless; I began to see people in a different light.... I found that my attitude to sport had changed. Previously, I had been very temperamental and aggressive. I still had the will to win, but now instead of giving knock for knock, I had no impulse to retaliate.

D. Read the following poem called 'The Jig-Saw':

Next time I won't start with the people, with the clear lines or the bright colours,
Next time I do a puzzle I'll do the sky first, or the trees, or the lawn, or the sea.
Those are always the parts that get left until last.
Yet the sky pieces matter as much as any others.
Without them the puzzle is incomplete.
How disappointing it is when even one piece of sky is missing and the puzzle can't be finished.

Lots of pieces, all different, all essential—fully-interlocking.
It's the same with a family, Lord, or a church or any other community.
No two members the same.
Some stand out; others are less obvious. But they all matter.
Each plays its part, each contributes, and all pieces lock together to form the whole.
If one is missing that whole is incomplete.

Whether I be sky, or grass, or tree, whether I be plain or brightly coloured, teach me to play my part well in whatever community I am, that others may rely on me. Lock me together with them to form a strong and satisfying whole.[2]

Ask pupils: 'What is the point the writer is trying to

get across in this poem?' Get pupils to explain the last line of the poem in the context of the whole poem.

E. Suggest pupils write a poem or prayer of their own on the theme: 'Life is like a Jigsaw'.

**IDEAS FOR DEVELOPMENT**
Get together with a science teacher and build a simple machine in which every screw and metal piece is needed.

**FOOTNOTES**

[1] 'Jane and Jill Powell: All-Round Sportswomen' in: John D. Searle, *On The Right Track—Contemporary Christians In Sport* (Marshall Pickering: Basingstoke, 1987), ISBN 0 551 01424 5, pp 119-134.

[2] 'The Jig-Saw' in: *The Christian Year—A Devotional Diary* (Foundary Press: London, 1987), ISBN 0 946550 08 5.

# 16

## THEME
# Water

**AIM**

To think about the different uses of water: ie its preciousness to life, its power to take and save life and its cleansing power.

**INTRODUCTION**

Produce a bottle of rain water or water from a river or canal—ask if anyone would like to drink it! Talk about the difficulties involved in getting pure drinking water when travelling abroad to certain countries. Some pupils may have experience of this. Suggest ways of coping with the problem of getting drinking water (eg boiling water, bottled water, water filters). Bring out the point that water may look clean but can be already polluted. Pure water can be a life-saver, polluted water can kill.

**OPTIONS AND IDEAS**

A. Fill a glass with ordinary tap water. Invite someone to drink it. Then put a drop of ink in the water. Would they still drink it? Ask: 'What could be done to reverse the damage produced by the ink?' Pour the dirty water out and fill the glass with fresh water, but make sure that some drops of dirty water are still in the glass so that the water will be coloured again. Would they drink it now? Stress the importance of cleaning and rinsing the glass thoroughly before pouring in some water to drink. Stress the importance of having pure water to drink for physical health, then compare this with the Christian idea of needing 'the water of life' for spiritual health (Revelation 22:17). Invite suggestions about who or what is this 'water of life' and where to get it. Point to the fact that Christians believe that Jesus himself is the 'water of life' because faith in him is the source of everlasting life. See John 4:13-14.

B. Working together in pairs, ask pupils to make a list of the many different uses of water (eg drinking, washing, hydro-electric power, cooling car engines, etc). Tell them to include fun things like swimming, garden ponds, fountains, etc. Still in pairs, ask pupils to estimate how much water on average they use in one day. Put these 'Water Fax' on an OHP to help them in their calculations:

> The body of an average adult male contains nearly 38 litres of water.
> We need to drink at least 2 litres of water a day.
> We can survive for up to 40 days without food but only three days without water.
> Although over 70% of the world's surface is covered by water, only 1% of this is fresh water suitable for drinking and irrigation.
> Every day, about 25,000 people die from diseases spread by drinking or using bad water.
> People in the UK use:
> —22 litres each time a toilet is flushed.
> —130 litres each, every day of their life.

Industry in the UK uses:
— 150,000 litres to produce a ton of steel.
— 168 litres for one Sunday newspaper.[1]

Ask pupils to think about how they could cut down their own use of water.

C. In some countries of the world there are severe problems because of drought, poor irrigation or polluted water. Some organisations work to relieve such situations. Here is one true story with a happy ending:

> Zwmoo Reriya, her husband Constati Jumamuni and three of their six children live in a small mud house in the village of Bukiringi in North East Zaire. Like most people in the area, Constati farms a small plot of land from which he reaps a modest harvest of sweet potatoes, cassava, maize, beans, tomatoes and peanuts. Their water supply, until a few years ago, was the stream in the valley which was used to provide their family's cooking, washing and drinking water. This same water source also served as a repository for human and animal waste, and so was a source of sickness and disease. The people suffered from intestinal worms and diarrhoea, and diseases like malaria, polio and typhoid spread rapidly through use of such polluted water. Over the years, people build up some resistance to the worst effects of polluted water, but young children are particularly vulnerable to disease before they are able to build up such immunity. A few years ago, the Anglican Church's Community Development Team based at Boga (20 kilometres to the South of Bukiringi) initiated a water improvement programme in the area, and Tim Rous, a water engineer with the Church Missionary Society helped local people to install a water filter system. It

only cost around £100, but it improved the health of thousands of people in that area.[2]

Find out how this system operates.[3] Ask pupils to imagine themselves as one of Zwmoo and Constati's children. Ask them to write about the difference the new water system has made to their village and their family.

## IDEAS FOR DEVELOPMENT

Look out for press cuttings about floods and droughts and consider ways of giving help.

Follow-up with the video, filmstrip or OHP pack from Tear Fund which illustrate their involvement in water development programmes in the Third World.[4]

## FOOTNOTES

[1] 'Water Fax' in: Tear Fund, *On Target* Issue 21, undated.
[2] Adapted from: John Capon, 'Water Of Life' in: Tear Fund, *Tear Times* Issue 43, Spring 1989, pp 2-4.
[3] On Target, *op cit* pp 3-4.
Simon Jenkins, *A World Of Difference* (Lion Publishing: Tring, 1988), ISBN 0 7459 1337 7, p 17.
[4] *Water Of Life* (Tear Fund: Teddington, undated). Available as video, filmstrip or OHP pack (with additional worship and display material). It provides a beautiful visual stimulus to meditate on God's provision of water for our needs as well as the problems created by polluted water in the Third World, and how Tear Fund helps to improve the quality and accessibility of water supplies. Duration: fifteen minutes.

# 17

## THEME
# The Senses

**AIM**
    i) To consider ways in which our senses contribute to the enjoyment and appreciation of life.
    ii) To heighten awareness of the wonders of our world.

**INTRODUCTION**
    On separate pieces of paper write the words: sight, hearing, smell, taste, touch. Five pupils are then chosen to mime the sense they are given to the rest of the group.

**OPTIONS AND IDEAS**

A. Share (either by bringing items in or by talking about them) some favourite pictures, sounds (a piece of music?), smells (a perfume or aftershave), tastes or things that are pleasant or interesting to touch (eg a smooth piece of wood, a piece of velvet or even a musical instrument like a keyboard or typewriter).

B. Prepare a tape of various sounds—some easy to guess and others more difficult. Use this as a basis for a 'sound quiz'. Reveal what they are at the end and see who has the highest score.

C. Rule out five columns with the five senses as headings. Get pupils to list some of their favourite things under the headings.

D. Ask pupils to try to imagine what it would be like not to be able to see or hear. The following poem by John Milton may be suitable to use with older pupils as stimulus material:

> O loss of sight, of thee I most complain!
> Blind among enemies, O worse than chains,
> Dungeon, or beggary, or decrepit age!
> Light, the prime work of God, to me is extinct,
> And all her various objects of delight
> Annulled, which might in part my grief have eased,
> Inferior to the vilest now become
> Of man or worm; the vilest here excel me,
> They creep, yet see; I, dark in light, exposed
> To daily fraud, contempt, abuse and wrong,
> Within doors, or without, still as a fool,
> In power of others, never in my own;
> Scarce half I seem to live, dead more than half.
> O dark, dark, dark, amid the blaze of noon,
> Irrecoverably dark, total eclipse
> Without all hope of day![1]

E. Younger pupils may like to draw eyes, ears, hands, a nose and a mouth and write their own prayer or poem on this theme.

F. This extract from the Ulrich Schaffer poem 'You Are' may be used to provoke discussion.

I hear you
   in the cry of the gull
   in the wind chasing the last leaves to fall
   in the whisper of a child
I see you
   in the animal shapes of cumulus clouds
   in the trees ten times my age
   in the wrinkled face of a woman over ninety
I taste you
   in the sweetness of whole wheat in black bread
   in the smooth richness of an avocado
   in the creek water from a cupped hand
I smell you
   in the air after a cleansing rain
   in the freshly cut green onion
   in the thick carpet of autumn leaves
I touch you
   in the smooth bark of a white birch
   in the rock beneath the summit tearing my hands
   in the texture of wet and dry sand

Lord teach me to hear and to see
Teach me to taste to smell and to touch
and teach me to read
to read your handwriting
your letters to me[2]

Ask: 'Who is the "You" in the poem?' Pupils may think about the meaning and content of this piece or use it to formulate a prayer.

## IDEAS FOR DEVELOPMENT

Contact may be made with either the national headquarters or a local branch of one of the organisations concerned with the blind or deaf.[3] A visitor to talk to an assembly group may be appropriate.

## FOOTNOTES

[1] John Milton, 'O Loss Of Sight' from: *Samson Agonistes*
In: John Wain (ed), *The Oxford Library Of English Poetry* (Guild Publishing: London, 1987), p 322.

[2] Abridged from the poem: 'You Are' in: Ulrich Schaffer, *Into Your Light* (Inter-Varsity Press: Leicester, 1979), ISBN 0 85110 626 9, p 43.

[3] National Deaf Children's Society, 45 Hereford Road, London W2 5AH, Tel: 071-2299272.

Royal Association in Aid of Deaf People, 27 Oak Road, Acton, London W3 7HN, Tel: 081-7436187.

Royal Commonwealth Society for the Blind, PO Box 191, Haywards Heath, West Sussex, RH16 1FN, Tel: 0444-412424.

Royal National Institute for the Blind, 224 Great Portland Street, London W1, Tel: 071-3881266.

Royal National Institute for the Deaf, 105 Gower Street, London WC1E 6AH, Tel: 071-3878033.

Guide Dogs for the Blind Association, Alexandra House, 9 Park Street, Windsor, Berks SL4 1GR, Tel: 0753-855711.

# 18

## THEME
# Habits

**AIM**
  i) To reflect on good and bad habits.
  ii) To show that bad habits are hard to break and to consider the Christian claim that Jesus can free people.

**INTRODUCTION**
Ask pupils how physically strong they reckon themselves to be and who the strongest person is in the group. Get the 'strongest' person out and tie a piece of thread around them so that both arms are pinned to their side. (Make sure the pupil is wearing a blazer or top coat to avoid the thread cutting into them.) Invite them to break free. This is easy, but see what happens when you have put ten and then twenty strands of thread around them. Make the point that bad habits get progressively harder to break.

## OPTIONS AND IDEAS

A. Make a list of things that pupils regard as bad habits. Ask: 'What makes a habit bad?' Discuss how bad habits and wrong behaviour can hurt other people.

B. Read Paul's words which were written when he was struggling to overcome personal failings:

> I don't understand myself at all, for I really want to do what is right, but I can't. I do what I don't want to—what I hate. I know perfectly well that what I am doing is wrong, and my bad conscience proves that I agree with these laws I am breaking. When I want to do good, I don't; and when I try not to do wrong, I do it anyway. Oh, what a terrible predicament I'm in! Who will free me from my slavery to this deadly lower nature? Thank God! It has been done by Jesus Christ our Lord. He has set me free (Romans 7:15-16,19,24-25).

Christians believe that the Holy Spirit comes to live inside them and that he changes them and gives them the power to break free from bad habits and wrong behaviour. Reflect on the meaning of these passages from the Bible:

> And I will give you a new heart—I will give you new and right desires—and put a new spirit within you. I will take out your stony hearts of sin and give you new hearts of love. And I will put my Spirit within you so that you will obey my laws and do whatever I command (Ezekiel 36:26-27).

> But when the Holy Spirit controls our lives he will produce this kind of fruit in us: love, joy, peace, patience, kindness, goodness, faithfulness, gentleness and self-control (Galatians 5:22-23).

C. Refer back to some of the bad habits listed earlier and discuss some practical ways of trying to overcome these. Point out that some people turn to prayer in an attempt to gain the strength they need to overcome their bad habits. Give opportunity for pupils to use the following prayer in a moment of silence:

> Dear God,
> About these habits I've got.
> Help me to kick them.
> Some are only little things,
> like biting my nails.
> But I don't want to be a slave to anything.
> Help me to look after my body.
> It seems stupid to neglect it.
> It's one of the things I've got going for me
> so why spoil it?
> I don't want to be a fitness freak;
> all I'm asking is
> that you give me common sense
> and the determination to follow it through.
> Oh, by the way,
> that goes for my head too.
> The habits in my thinking.
> Keep my mind clean;
> don't let me waste my time on selfish daydreams.
> Help me not to judge things
> before I've looked at the evidence
> and not to be biassed when I do.
> It's so easy to be prejudiced about all sorts of things.
> I know beliefs can't be proved, Lord,
> that's what faith's all about;
> but help me to know inside myself
> what to believe.
> I'm always asking your help, Lord,
> that's becoming a habit.

It's one worth having, I suppose.
I pray that it will never become just an empty habit.
Shake me up if it does.[1]

D. Think about some habits which are good and can have positive results. Group them under three headings, ie habits which have positive effects on: (a) myself, (b) others, (c) the world at large. Give some examples to start the discussion, eg bathing regularly (this may belong under more than one heading!), taking empty bottles to the bottle bank, reading the Bible every day.

E. Point out that bad habits can ruin a life. All too often people look back when they are older and regret some of the things they did which affected their lives in a negative way. Christians believe, however, that God has the power to enable them to make something of themselves. Bad habits can be overcome. The following inscription was written by a Christian and illustrates the belief that God is making something better from the rubble of his life. Read this and then ask pupils: 'If your life were a building, what would be written on the plaque?':

> To God, the designer; who laid the foundation before the world began.
> It got a bit mucked about in the construction process; but
> restoration work is now in progress, and
> In time God will complete it.

Get pupils to design a plaque of their own.

## IDEAS FOR DEVELOPMENT

Collect together some stories about people who have found release from their bad habits when they put themselves under God's ruling, eg the stories about drug addicts from Hong Kong's

Walled City who got into contact with Jackie Pullinger's work among them. You could watch clips of the documentary about her work.[2]

**FOOTNOTES**

[1] Janet Green, *Home-made Prayers* (Lion Publishing: Tring, 1983), ISBN 0 85848 211 0, p 36.
[2] Jackie Pullinger, *Crack In The Wall—Life & Death In Kowloon Walled City* (Hodder & Stoughton: Sevenoaks, 1989), ISBN 0 340 48807 7.
*The Law Of Love* (CTVC, Beeson's Yard, Bury Lane, Rickmansworth, Herts WD3 1DS, 1990). Video. Duration: two hours.

# 19

## THEME
# Food And Feasting

**AIM**
  i) To consider the importance and significance attached to certain foods and feasting.
  ii) To think about the religious significance of certain feasts in Judaism and in Christianity.

**INTRODUCTION**
Arrange a tasting competition. Blindfold volunteers one at a time, then give each a spoon to taste a selection of prepared foods. The correct answers are revealed at the end and a small reward given to the pupil with the highest score.

**OPTIONS AND IDEAS**

A. Talk about the important role food plays in our everyday lives (ie the money spent on it, the huge range available in the shops, the time spent preparing it). Refer to times when meals bring families and friends together (eg birthday teas, anniversaries, weddings, christenings, etc). Invite pupils to share their experiences and either design menus appropriate to these different occasions or one for a meal they particularly remember.

B. Point out that feasting, eating and drinking have always been considered appropriate ways of celebrating certain events and a socially acceptable way of enjoying oneself. The people of ancient Rome were no exception. A wealthy Roman citizen could select a menu which used a variety of foods from their vast empire. The *cena* (dinner) would start around 4 pm and often continue into the night. Guests reclined at a *triclinium* (three couches) and were served at portable tables which would be changed at the end of the various courses. Prepare an OHP of the menu for Trimalchio's feast to show pupils:

*Gustatio* (Hors d'oeuvres)
White and black olives.
Dormice sprinkled with honey and poppy seeds.
Grilled sausages.
Damsons and pomegranate seeds.
Beccaficos in spiced egg yolk.
Honeyed wine.

*Fercula* (Prepared dishes)
Foods of the Zodiac served on a round plate (on the sign of the Ram, chick-peas; on the Bull, beef; on the Twins, kidneys; on the Crab, a crown of myrtle; on the Lion, African figs; on the Virgin, a sterile sow's womb; on the Balance, scales supporting tarts and honey cakes; on the Scorpion, a scorpion fish; on the Archer, an eyefish; on the Goat's horns, a lobster; on the Waterbearer, a goose; on the Fishes, two red mullets) served with bread and surrounding: Roasted fattened fowls, sow bellies, and hare. Roast whole wild boar with dates, suckled by piglets made of cakes and stuffed with live thrushes.

Boiled whole pig stuffed with sausage and black puddings.

With the fercula served Falernian wine 100 years old.

*Mensae secundae* (Dessert)
Fruits and cakes.
Boned, fattened chickens and goose eggs.
Pastries stuffed with raisins and nuts.
Quince-apples and pork disguised as fowls and fish.
Oysters and scallops.
Snails.[1]

Put pupils in pairs. One of them is to imagine that they were a guest at the feast and they have to describe the meal to their partner.

C. The Jews celebrate the festival of Passover by eating a special *Seder* meal. It reminded them that God freed them from their captivity in Egypt. Read the account of the preparations for Jesus' last Passover meal with his disciples in Mark 14:12–16. Study the list of foods eaten at such a meal, then ask pupils to draw some of the foods which can then be cut out and mounted to form a collage:

—Lamb: eaten roasted, or sometimes as sop (thinned out with vegetables like a stew).
—Unleavened bread: flat loaves made of wheat or barley flour, salt and water.
—Wine: four glasses of diluted wine (representing the four phases of redemption in Egypt—Exodus 6:6–7).
—Bitter herbs: onions, garlic, radishes, peppers, etc (representing the cruel bondage in Egypt).
—Haroseth: contains ground apples, raisins, figs,

nuts, wine and honey (resembling the mud mortar of Egyptian bondage).
- Eggs: baked at 300°F for 45 minutes (an ancient symbol of suffering).
- Parsley and salt water (representing the angels' tears for the Egyptians who lost their lives in the Red Sea).
- Grapes, raisins, dates, figs, prunes, apricots.
- Almonds, walnuts, wheat, barley, carob or seeds.
- Honey, olives, pickles, cucumbers, cheese, dried fish.

D. Jesus celebrated this Passover feast with his disciples just before he was arrested, tried and put to death. At this meal he instituted what is now known as The Lord's Supper or Holy Communion or Eucharist. To this day, Christians all over the world celebrate this event regularly. The Communion is a time of fellowship, when together Christians remember Jesus' death and sacrifice for humankind. It is also a meal of reconciliation and unity which looks forward to the coming of Jesus in triumph. These are the words with which Jesus introduced the 'breaking of bread and wine':

> 'This is my body, given for you. Eat it in remembrance of me.... This wine is the token of God's new agreement to save you—an agreement sealed with the blood I shall pour out to purchase back your souls' (Luke 22:19-20).

## IDEAS FOR DEVELOPMENT

Invite pupils to bring in one item of food for a 'First Century Passover Meal'. Arrange a time when these foods can be shared together.

Ask Christians from different Christian churches and denominations about the way in which they celebrate the Eucharist.

## FOOTNOTE

[1] 'Trimalchio's Feast' in: John Edwards, *The Roman Cookery Of Apicius* (Century Hutchinson: London, 1984), ISBN 0 7126 1064 2, p xix.

# 20

## THEME

# It's A Miracle!

**AIM**

    i) To think about what a miracle really is.
    ii) To help pupils understand that some Christians believe that they can happen today.

**INTRODUCTION**

Show the group this simple magic trick:

> Confuse your audience with a specially prepared egg, which you have soaked in strong vinegar for two days and taken out of the solution just before the demonstration. Place your egg amongst some ordinary ones, but be careful to remember which one it is. Take the special egg and tell the audience that by throwing the egg with superior skill it is possible to make it bounce. After your successful egg-bouncing, some other people may want to test their skill![1]

Ask: 'Is this a miracle or just a trick or skill someone has learnt?'.

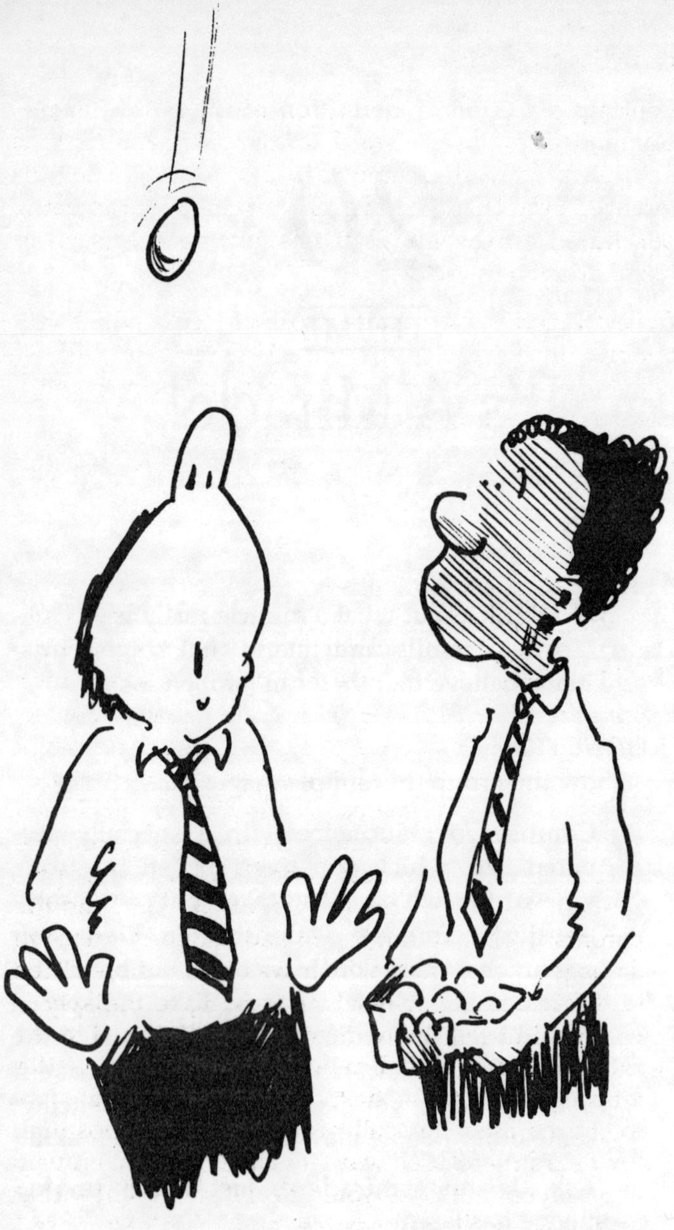

## OPTIONS AND IDEAS

A. Look up a dictionary definition of the word 'magic'. Compare it with the word 'miracle'. Ask questions like: 'Are they the same thing?' 'What is the difference?' Add that we have all seen magic tricks being performed on the TV—but has anyone ever seen or heard about a miracle?

B. Collect together any available news items which talk about 'miracle rescues' or 'miracle cures', etc. Discuss whether or not they are real miracles or 'lucky escapes' or the result of human cleverness.

C. Read the true story of Karen, told by Pam Richardson:

> One Saturday night in May 1967, a couple from our church came to our home. They were in deep distress. Their three month old baby girl, Karen, was dangerously ill and in Great Ormond Street Hospital. Her parents had rushed her there on Friday, and on arrival Karen was found to have a very high temperature. She was placed in intensive care, where she had a series of fits which left her right side paralysed. After a lot of investigations the doctors said that the nearest diagnosis they could get was a rare form of meningitis (later diagnosed as encephalitis), and again antibiotics were prescribed. A brain scan was then carried out, and the parents were told that Karen had suffered extensive damage to the brain which was irreversible. They said that if she lived—which was highly unlikely— she would be severely mentally handicapped to the extent that it was indicated that it would be better for Karen to die. The next day our friends came late to church after their all-night vigil at the hospital. We heard that Karen was still alive but dangerously ill. I prayed that God would heal Karen. I knew that I was asking the impossible, and I don't suppose I

really expected any reply, but just then I sensed God saying to me: 'You are asking me to heal Karen just like you would ask someone to pass the jam across the table'. Then I felt God's challenge within me (I was expecting my third child at the time): 'Would you do anything, give everything...even the life of your own unborn child?' At that moment in time I answered 'Yes'. By now everyone in the church was praying for baby Karen. I felt that I must go to Karen's mother and take her to the front of the church to kneel at the Holy Communion table. Being a rather shy person I found that a difficult thing to do but I managed it somehow. Kneeling there with Karen's mother with our open hands on the Communion table, a great peace came over me and I felt that all would be well and Karen would live. It was just after 12 o'clock. At around 12.15 pm when Karen's parents went out to telephone the hospital, they were told that they should come immediately as something was happening with Karen. It turned out that at 12 o'clock the nurse had called the doctor because she could find no trace of Karen's pulse. As she was just about to cover her over as dead, there was a flicker, a tremor of movement in her right side and all day Karen continued to regain the use of her right side. The next day another reading of the brain was taken with the same machine used before. It registered 'no brain damage'. This was impossible. As yet there is no way damaged brain cells can be repaired. So another scan was ordered but the result was the same. Not only had the baby survived but the impossible had happened; she would not be mentally handicapped as the doctors had predicted two days before. After a week of observation, Karen was sent home. She continued to go back to the hospital for the rest of the year for regular check-ups until the doctors said that it was pointless bringing such a healthy, happy child to the hospital. They called Karen 'the miracle baby' because they had no medical explanation for what had happened.

Point out that for some people this true story represents a real miracle. Ask: 'What do you think?' 'What other explanation could there be for Karen's recovery?'

D. Explain that many Christians believe in a God who can, at any time, intervene or step in to do a miracle and to heal people who are sick. The New Testament has many stories about Jesus performing miracles. One of Jesus' greatest miracles was probably the resurrection of Lazarus who had already been dead for three days. Find the story in John 11:1–48.

## IDEAS FOR DEVELOPMENT

Ask the pupils to write down one miracle they would really like to happen.

Collect stories about modern miracles.

**FOOTNOTE**
[1] 'Rubbery Egg' in: Sally Kindberg, *Tricky Tricks* (Lutterworth Press: Cambridge, 1986), ISBN 0 7188 2654 X, pp 10-11.

# 21

## THEME

# Don't Blame Me!

**AIM**

To provoke thought about the negative implications of wrong-doing and the reluctance to accept blame.

**INTRODUCTION**

Here are some statements taken from insurance claim forms. They are actual examples of car drivers' attempts to excuse themselves and avoid taking the blame for a motor accident.

'My car was legally parked as it backed into the other vehicle.'
'An invisible car came out of nowhere, struck my car and vanished.'
'Coming home I drove into the wrong house and collided with a tree I don't have.'
'A pedestrian hit me and went under my car.'
'I thought my window was down, but I found out it was up when I put my head through it.'

'I collided with a stationary truck coming the other way.'

'In an attempt to kill a fly, I drove into a telephone pole.'

'The pedestrian had no idea which way to run, so I ran over him.'

'I was thrown from my car as it left the road. I was later found in a field by some stray cows.'

'As I approached the intersection a sign suddenly appeared in a place where no stop sign had ever appeared before. I was unable to stop in time to avoid the accident.'[1]

Ask: 'Why do you think the people came up with these excuses?' 'Why were they so anxious to give the impression it was not their fault?'

## OPTIONS AND IDEAS

A. Arrange pupils in pairs to discuss the following questions: (a) 'Can you remember an occasion when you tried to blame someone else for something?' (b) 'Why do we find it so difficult to face up to our own mistakes?' (c) 'What would have happened if you had accepted the blame?' (d) 'Is it all right to make up excuses or blame others for something you know to be your fault? Why/why not?'

B. Ask pupils to define the term 'white lie'. Compare definitions, then ask: 'Is there really such a thing or are all attempts to disguise the truth equally dishonest?'

C. The Bible depicts great and famous people such as King David in an honest light. He was called a 'man after God's own heart' despite the fact that he did a terrible thing. Here is part of the story: Once David fell in love with Bathsheba, the wife of an army captain and summoned her to his palace for the night. She became pregnant and he tried to cover up his adultery by devious means but failed. He arranged for Bathsheba's husband Uriah, to be killed in battle, and brought the widow back to his palace and married her himself. Then the prophet Nathan paid David a visit. Read the 'Nathan Rap' which is based on 2 Samuel 12:1–14. The last line is to be taken poetically and not literally: David did not die but his son, born from Bathsheba, did.

> It was evening in the palace when the prophet came by,
> There was trouble in his manner, there was thunder in his eye,
> He was still for a moment, he was framed in the door,
> And the king said, 'Nathan!...What are you here for?'
> The prophet said, 'David, I've a tale to tell,'
> So the king sat and listened as the darkness fell,
> While the hard-eyed prophet took a seat and began,
> The story of a merciless and evil man.
>
> 'This man,' said Nathan, 'had a mountain of gold,
> Sheep by the thousand he bought and sold,
> He never said, 'Can I afford it or not?'
> What this man wanted, this man got!
> And one thing he wanted, and he wanted real bad,
> Was the only living thing that a poor man had,
> And he knew that it was wrong, but he took it just the same.'
> 'I'll kill him!' said the king, 'Just tell me his name!'
>
> Then a silence fell upon them like the silence of a tomb,
> The prophet nodded slowly as he moved across the room,
> And, strangely, as he came he grew more awesome and more wise,

And when he looked at David there was sadness in his eyes.
But David's anger burned in him, he drew his sword and said,
'I swear, before the dawn has come, that sinner will be dead!
No more delay, no mercy talk, give me his name!' he cried,
Then Nathan said, 'It's you, it's you!' and the king just died.[2]

D. Guide pupils to think about the merits of 'owning up' and admitting before God and people that we have done something wrong. Look up Psalm 32 or Psalm 51 and read what King David wrote after this encounter with Nathan, the prophet. Give an opportunity for pupils to quietly reflect on one of these psalms.

**IDEAS FOR DEVELOPMENT**

Design an 'Honesty Quiz' based on common situations most of us have faced (eg What do you do when you damage something you have borrowed? Do you (a) say it was already like that when you borrowed it, (b) hope no one notices, (c) own up and offer to replace it).

**FOOTNOTES**

[1] Abridged from: 'Autocover Insurance (1) in: Linda Hoy/Mike Hoy, *An Alternative Assembly Book* (Longman: Harlow, 1985), ISBN 0 582 36124 9, pp 1,10.

[2] Abridged from: 'Nathan Rap' in: Adrian Plass, *Clearing Away The Rubbish* (Minstrel/Monarch Publications: Eastbourne, 1988), ISBN 1 85424 025 0, pp 184-185.

# 22

## THEME

# Getting To Know You

**AIM**
    i) To consider how well we know each other.
    ii) To think about God's knowledge of people.

**INTRODUCTION**
Arrange for pupils to bring in a photograph of themselves as a baby. Number these and place them around the room. See how many pupils they can identify.

**OPTIONS AND IDEAS**

A. Ask the group to say why they recognised some people, but failed to recognise others. Discuss some of the things that make people instantly recognisable (eg colour of hair, eyes, shape of their noses, their voice, etc).

B. Without the rest of the group knowing and with the aid of three willing pupils, compile short profiles on them. Read these out and ask the class to guess whom you are describing.

C. Discuss how well we really know each other, even those we regard as our best friends. Call out two friends who are willing to try a game to see how well they know each other. Ask A to go out of the room while you ask B three questions, eg: 'What is A's favourite food?' 'What does A most like to do in spare time?' 'What colour eyes has A got?' Bring A back and ask the same questions and compare answers. B can then be sent out and the exercise could be repeated with the same or a different set of questions.

D. Working in pairs, ask pupils to draw up two personal profiles, one of themselves and one of each other. Get them to swap these and compare them. Ask which profile is nearest to the truth? Discuss: 'Do our best friends know everything about us?' 'Are there some things we wouldn't want even our best friends to know?'

E. Explain that Christians believe that Jesus knows everything about us. He was able to tell a lady from Samaria whom he had never met before intimate details about her life. Here is the story:

> He had to go through Samaria on the way, and around noon as he approached the village of Sychar, he came to Jacob's Well, located on the parcel of ground Jacob gave to his son Joseph. Jesus was tired from the long walk in the hot sun and sat wearily beside the well. Soon a Samaritan woman came to draw water, and Jesus asked her for a drink. He was alone at the time as his disciples had gone into the village to buy some food. The woman was surprised that a Jew would ask a 'despised Samaritan' for anything—usually they wouldn't even speak to them!—and she remarked about this to Jesus. He replied, 'If you only knew what a wonderful gift God has for you, and who I am, you would ask me

for some living water!' 'Please, sir,' the woman said, 'give me some of that water! Then I'll never be thirsty again and won't have to make this long trip out here every day.' 'Go and get your husband,' Jesus told her. 'But I am not married,' the woman replied. 'All too true!' Jesus said. 'For you have had five husbands, and you aren't even married to the man you're living with now.' 'Sir,' the woman said, 'you must be a prophet.... Well, at least I know that the Messiah will come—the one they call Christ—and when he does, he will explain everything to us.' Then Jesus told her, 'I am the Messiah!' Just then his disciples arrived. They were surprised to find him talking to a woman, but none of them asked him why, or what they had been discussing. Then the woman left her waterpot beside the well and went back to the village and told everyone, 'Come and meet a man who told me everything I ever did! Can this be the Messiah?' (John 4:4–10,15–19,25–29).

Point out that Jews and Samaritans did not usually mix with each other, and certainly not with the opposite sex. Although Jesus did not approve of this woman's way of life, he did not condemn her, but shared with her the secret of who he really was. In the same way, Christians believe that although God knows all their faults he still loves them and wants them to know and love him too.

F. Discuss the idea contained in the following Bible references that God knows individuals in a way that even closest friends cannot know them:

And he knows the number of hairs on your head! (Luke 12:7).

For he knows everything we do (1 John 3:20b).

Some pupils may like to use this prayer:

> Lord, you know us better than we know ourselves. You know us from deep within. Often you don't approve of things we do or say but you are still loving us. Thank you that you are for us.

**IDEAS FOR DEVELOPMENT**
Think about practical ways of getting to know each other better.

# 23

## THEME
# Forgiveness

**AIM**

To show the importance of forgiving and being forgiven.

**INTRODUCTION**

Question: 'Have you ever found it difficult to forgive someone?' Invite contributions from pupils. Give a personal example.

**OPTIONS AND IDEAS**

A. Divide into groups of three or four. Discuss these questions: (a) 'Is it always possible to forgive people, even if they have done something terrible?' (b) 'Is it ever right not to forgive someone?' (c) 'Can you give some examples of when it would be difficult to forgive?'

B. Look at these true stories which show some people's ability to forgive those who have caused them and their families great suffering:

The Ealing vicar Michael Saward publicly forgave the attackers who broke into his home and raped his daughter in front of him and savagely beat her boyfriend and himself with a cricket bat. Later, the rape victim herself joined the congregation of St Mary's Church in Ealing praying, 'We wish that those who did these crimes may be punished, but we forgive them.'

Reverend Michael Counsell, a vicar from Birmingham, wrote to the hit-and-run driver who killed his five-year-old son Simon and later gave himself up, saying 'Every day when we say the Lord's prayer, we pray, "Forgive us our trespasses as we forgive those that trespass against us." I think I would choke over those words if I expected God to forgive me all the wrong things I have done, if I had not already forgiven you from my heart.' When the case came to court, it would appear that the forgiving attitude of Reverend and Mrs Counsell influenced the judge and resulted in the driver walking from the court with only a fine and a driving ban and not a prison sentence as he might easily have expected.[1]

Quietly think about the following points and write down your answers: (a) 'What do you think your attitude would be towards the driver of the car?' (b) 'How do you feel about Reverend and Mrs Counsell's reaction?'

A letter to the *Daily Mirror* written in relation to the Ealing Vicarage rape shows how one reader felt about what happened, it said: 'It's very Christian of the vicarage rape girl to pray for forgiveness for her attackers. But I can safely say if anyone raped either of my daughters I'd be praying for immediate revenge.'[2] Ask: 'What do you think about this?' 'Do you think you would want revenge if something like that happened to someone you cared about?'

C. Write up the following statements on the board.

> If I cannot feel forgiveness, then the very message for which I stand and preach as a Christian minister is empty (Michael Saward).

> It is natural to feel angry when our children are hurt but we must forgive—for our own sakes. Otherwise we will become consumed by hate and our lives will be intolerable (Michael Counsell).

Ask pupils to check them against the Bible passages:

> Never criticise or condemn—or it will all come back on you. Go easy on others; then they will do the same for you (Luke 6:37).

> Then Peter came to him [Jesus] and asked, 'Sir, how often should I forgive a brother who sins against me? Seven times?' 'No!' Jesus replied, 'seventy times seven!' (Matthew 18:21).

> Instead, be kind to each other, tender-hearted, forgiving one another, just as God has forgiven you because you belong to Christ (Ephesians 4:32).

> 'Father, forgive these people,' Jesus said, 'for they don't know what they are doing' (Luke 23:34).

> The Parable of the Unforgiving Servant (Matthew 18:21-35).

D. Silently contemplate the words of the poem 'Magnificent Obsession' by Phil Streeter. Do you believe in a God who forgives?

I know that You have forgiven me.
Not that I can
feel it—
see it—
prove it—
or at times even believe it!
But because You said so.
For as sure as
rivers shiver toward faraway seas,
stars creep out at night and
October follows apple-ripe September,
You will continue to indulge Yourself
in that overpowering, gluttonous,
extravagant obsession
of forgiving.[3]

## IDEAS FOR DEVELOPMENT

Do a project on Corrie Ten Boom, a survivor of the Nazi concentration camps, who had every right to be bitter and angry against the Germans but forgave them again and again.[4]

## FOOTNOTES

[1] Adapted from 'Forgive Us Our Trespasses As We Forgive Those...' in: *Buzz* May 1986, pp 32-37.
Jill Saward/Wendy Green, *Rape—My Story* (Bloomsbury Publishing: London, 1990), ISBN 0 7475 0751 1.

[2] From a letter to the *Daily Mirror* quoted in: *ibid*

[3] Phil Streeter, 'Magnificent Obsession' (1986).

[4] Corrie Ten Boom/John & Elizabeth Sherrill, *The Hiding Place* (Hodder & Stoughton, Sevenoaks, 1971), ISBN 0 340 20845 7, pp 220-221.
Kathleen White, *Corrie* (Marshall Pickering: Basingstoke, 1983), ISBN 0 551 01061 4.

# 24

## THEME

# Two-Way Communication

**AIM**   i) To show the importance of talking and listening in communication.
      ii) To consider prayer as a means of communicating with God.

## INTRODUCTION

Invite three of the 'best' talkers in the class to come to the front and try to talk non-stop for thirty seconds on a chosen topic (eg my hobby, my hero, etc). Ask the listeners what they can remember from these talks. Think about how well they listened. By a show of hands discover who would find it easier to talk than to listen.

## OPTIONS AND IDEAS

A. Divide the class into groups, and appoint a chairperson for each. Tell them that their task is to look at other ways in which people communicate with each other. Ask for some examples (varying tones of voice to express different moods, non-verbal communication such as yawning, etc) and let each group select one example to act out to the rest of the class.

B. Get the pupils into pairs and let them do the following exercise 'Destructive/Interruptive Listening': Pupil A talks about his or her favourite subject/hobby and pupil B expresses that s/he is not interested by yawning, looking away, fidgeting, etc or interrupts all the time in an attempt to lead the conversation. Swap after two minutes.[1] Ask: 'What did it feel like talking to somebody who is obviously not listening?' (That's what a lot of teachers experience every day!)

C. Explain that Christians see prayer as communication between God and themselves and involves both talking and listening. Choose two pupils to read this adapted version of the prayer Jesus taught the disciples:

—OUR FATHER IN HEAVEN...
—Yes?
—Don't interrupt me. I'm praying.
—But you were talking to me.
—Me? No, not really. OUR FATHER...
—See? You address me. So what's it about?
—HALLOWED BE YOUR NAME...
—Do you really mean it?
—What?
—Hallowing my name.
—What does that mean?
—It means honouring me—that I'm precious to you, that I'm No 1.
—Ah, right. YOUR KINGDOM COME, YOUR WILL BE DONE ON EARTH AS IT IS IN HEAVEN...
—And what are you doing for my kingdom? And are you doing my will?
—Well, I go to church sometimes.

—That's not enough. I want more. I want you to change your habit of bullying. I want you to be more concerned for other people than for yourself.
—Why do you always pick on me? What about Fred? He is doing the same, isn't he?
—Hold on! Weren't you just now praying that your whole life comes under my control as the King and that you would be able to do my will?
—All right, all right. Please can I finish my prayers now.
—GIVE US TODAY OUR DAILY BREAD...
—Would you be satisfied if I gave you only bread to eat! Come on, be honest. You even moan when vegetables are on your menu instead of chips or baked beans.
—FORGIVE US OUR SINS AS WE FORGIVE THOSE WHO SIN AGAINST US...
—What about Bob?
—Bob? Please don't start talking about Bob. Don't you know how he made a fool of me yesterday at school?
—Yes, I know. But you were just praying that...
—Oh, I didn't take it seriously.
—Well, at least you're honest. Are you enjoying walking around feeling cross and bitter about Bob?
—No, not really.
—I can help you. Just forgive Bob for what he's done to you and I will forgive you. I know it might cost you your reputation but only then, will you be at peace.
—Mmm, not sure if I can—after all he's done. AND LEAD US NOT INTO TEMPTATION, BUT DELIVER US FROM EVIL.
—I'd love to. Just keep away from situations and people who tempt you to think or do something which is wrong.
—I'm not with you.

- —You know only too well your weaknesses: bullying others, fantasising about girls, being lazy at school...
- —Puh! I think this was the most difficult prayer I've ever prayed. But at least it relates to my ordinary life.
- —Fine! We'll get there!
- —FOR YOURS IS THE KINGDOM, THE POWER AND THE GLORY FOR EVER. AMEN.
- —You know what? I really enjoy it when people like you start to take me seriously and have a real chat with me about things and do what I tell them to do.[2]

Ask: 'How important is prayer to a Christian?' and 'Is there more to prayer than just asking for things?'

D. The telephone provides the opportunity for two-way communication (talking and listening) and is often used to illustrate the Christian concept of communication with God. Prayer and Bible reading provide important lines of communication between God and humankind. Psalm 50:15 is sometimes called the telephone number for the 'hot line' to God. Look this up and suggest some pupils may like to write a 'telephone prayer', ie a prayer in the form of a telephone conversation. Give opportunity for pupils to use the prayer they have written or to listen to someone else reading their prayer aloud. Perhaps some prayers can be selected for use in a hall assembly.

## IDEAS FOR DEVELOPMENT

Collect information about some of the modern advances in communications (eg: fax, satellite TV, car phones, computer modems, etc). Decide which can be used to both give and receive information.

Make your own 'telephone' connecting two beakers with a string.

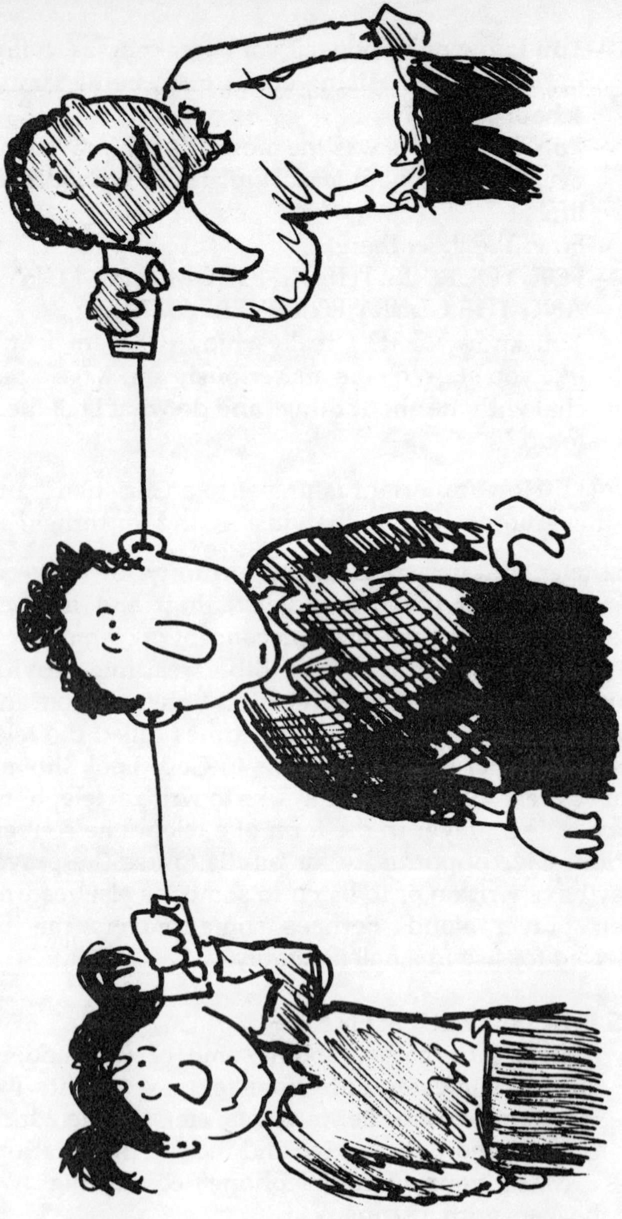

**FOOTNOTES**

[1] 'Destructive/Interruptive Listening' adapted from: Jim Wingate, *How To Be A Peace-full Teacher* (Pilgrims Publications: Canterbury, 1985), ISBN 0 948728 14 0, p 11.

[2] 'Please, Lord, Don't Interrupt Me I'm Praying' adapted from an unknown German source.

# 25

## THEME

# A Time To Remember

**AIM**
   i) To reflect on past events and ways of recording these.
   ii) To think about the importance of the Bible to Christians as a record of past events.

**INTRODUCTION**
   Use a clip from a video which depicts highlights from a particular year in modern history.[1]

**OPTIONS AND IDEAS**

A. Discuss various ways of recording information about important internal or international events (ie TV, radio, newspaper, tapes and film). Newspaper clippings may be selected to provide an example.

B. Show or talk about a large variety of diaries available on the market. Many politicians and famous people keep diaries with a view to publication later in life (eg Tony Benn). Ask how many pupils have diaries and to what extent they use them. Talk about the kind of information most people would put in their diary. Think about some famous diaries, give some examples, eg *The Diary Of Anne Frank*, *The Secret Diary Of Adrian Mole*, *The Diary Of An Edwardian Lady*, etc. Find an extract from *The Diary Of Anne Frank* which will illustrate how diaries can give valuable insight into peoples' lives and thoughts.[2]

C. Study the extract from T. E. Herbert's biography based on events recorded in his diary while serving in the First World War. Point out that Mr Herbert was only a few years older than them (nineteen years old) when he went off to war.

> I can recall feeling a bit apprehensive while travelling in the RFC tender on my way to the line, I really didn't know what to expect, but things were going to be worse than anything I could imagine. We stopped at a big notice at the roadside which said 'Gas masks at the alert beyond this point'. So we did what was necessary and moved on. Very soon now we were in a lunar landscape. As far as the eye could see the earth was pock-marked with shell holes, and all were full of stinking stagnant water. Where once had been woods or clumps of trees only charred stumps were to be seen. Not a building could be seen anywhere, all had been destroyed. We were now well amongst the artillery, each gun hidden away in a cover of wire netting camouflage. How anyone ever found their way to any particular point always amazed me out here, I would have been completely lost.... I reported to the Battery Commander, and then met the RFC operator who was already there. I, apparently was a replacement for a casualty.... The Battery was a Yorkshire one, having been formed in the Barnsley area, and the dialect was pretty strong. The only 'foreigners'

among them, some from London and elsewhere, were replacements. One of the first things to strike me was that they all looked so unkempt and dirty. I was inclined to write them off as a rough old lot of Yorkshire miners. There wasn't a miner among them. There were at least six schoolmasters, and many of the others held good jobs in civil life, which became obvious when they talked. Soon I would be as dirty and unkempt as the rest of them. The term 'dirty' also covers infestation with lice.[3]

Mr Herbert has called his biography *The Lost Years*. Give pupils a few moments to jot down their ideas about why he chose this title, then use these thoughts to stimulate discussion on the subject of soldiers' diaries as valuable sources of information and personal reflection during times of war.

D. Tell the group that they have been given the task of producing a video in the *Year To Remember* series to show the highlights of the previous year. About which events would they include information and pictures?

E. Explain that to many people, the Bible is a unique record and commentary on events of religious significance. The Gospels, for example, provide an important record of the life of Jesus, and Christians see Christmas and Easter as times to remember particularly significant events in his life. Pupils could try to write up a suitable biblical story in diary form, eg a day in the life of Jesus from a disciple's perspective. Use Mark 1:16–34 for this task. Alternatively, write up the 'seven days of creation'. Here is an idea to get them started:

| Mon Jan 1st | Made a good start by separating light and darkness. Decided to call it 'day and night'. |
| --- | --- |
| Tues Jan 2nd | Got rather wet today dividing water. Gave the name 'sea' to one lot and 'sky' to another. |

Use the text from Genesis 1:1—2:4 to help complete this diary.

## IDEAS FOR DEVELOPMENT

As a class project work out what events in the school calendar could provide material for a 'Year To Remember' school video project over the coming year.

## FOOTNOTES

[1] *A Year To Remember Series* (Parkfield Entertainment: 1990). Available from some local video shops.
[2] Anne Frank, *The Diary Of Anne Frank* (Pan Books: London, 1954), ISBN 0 330 10737 2.
[3] T. E. Herbert, *The Lost Years* (unpublished).

# 26

## THEME
# Hope

**AIM**

To explore the Christian belief that their hope of life after death is certain.

**INTRODUCTION**

Read out a number of these inscriptions from tombstones in the Cambridge City cemetery and discuss which, if any, reflect the hope of a life after death and which are simply expressions of grief.

(a) God saw that you were suffering.
He knew you needed rest.
His garden must be beautiful.
He only takes the best.

(b) Reunited.

(c) In sure and certain hope of the resurrection.

(d) Death is only a shadow across the path to heaven.

(e) Dry up your tears and do not weep.
My sufferings now are past.
You gave to me your kindest aid.
So long as life did last.

(f) Departed to be with Christ.

## OPTIONS AND IDEAS

A. Explain that Christians believe that death is a consequence of the presence of evil in this world, but it is not the end because Jesus won the victory over death when he rose from the dead. This is the hope of every Christian. Put pupils into pairs. Ask them to work together to invent a situation in which they know they will win, but the final whistle hasn't yet blown! (Example: In a game of chess a point is reached when one player knows for certain that they will win, but the game still has to be finished). Some pupils could share their ideas with the rest of the group perhaps in a mime or short drama. Use this to illustrate that Christian hope is certain. Christians can be sure that life is stronger than death, love stronger than hate, joy stronger than pain and suffering.

B. Read the following extracts from *The Last Battle* by C. S. Lewis.[1] Explain that this is an account of the children from *The Chronicles Of Narnia* approaching a door (death) and reaching heaven—escaping from the bounds of the 'Shadowlands' (life on earth):

> 'I feel in my bones,' said Poggin, 'that we shall all, one by one, pass through that dark door before morning. I can think of a hundred deaths I would rather have died.' 'It is indeed a grim door,' said Tirian. 'It is more like a mouth.' 'Oh, can't we do anything to stop it?' said Jill in a shaken voice. 'Nay, fair friend,' said Jewel, nosing her gently. 'It may be

for us the door to Aslan's country and we shall sup at his table tonight' (pp 122-123).

After the children have come through the door they explore 'heaven':

> 'Listen, Peter. When Aslan said you could never go back to Narnia, he meant the Narnia you were thinking of. But that was not the real Narnia. That had a beginning and an end. It was only a shadow or a copy of the real Narnia which has always been here and always will be here: just as our own world, England and all, is only a shadow or a copy of something in Aslan's real world. And of course it is different; as different as a real thing is from a shadow or as waking life is from a dream' (pp 160-161).

> 'All their life in this world and all their adventures in Narnia had only been the cover and the title page: now at last they were beginning Chapter One of the Great Story which no one on earth has read: which goes on forever: in which every chapter is better than the one before' (p 173).

C. Look up the Bible passages: John 14:1–4 and Revelation 21:2–5 and compare them with David Watson's words before his death. He was an Anglican vicar from York who had cancer and died peacefully on February 18th 1984.

> In the first week of January 1984:
> Whatever else is happening to me physically, God is working deeply in my life. His challenge to me can be summed up in three words: 'Seek my face.' I am not now clinging to physical life (though I still believe that God can heal and wants to heal); but I am clinging to the Lord. I am ready to go and to be with Christ forever. That would be literally heaven.

But I'm equally ready to stay, if that is what God wants. 'Father, not my will but yours be done.' In that position of security I have experienced once again his perfect love, a love that casts out all fear.

On January 8th in a sermon:
Even death itself is not a threat.

On January 30th to a close friend:
I am completely at peace—there is nothing that I want more than to go to heaven. I know how good it is.

On Friday evening, 17th February to his wife:
I'm very tired; let's go home.[2]

## IDEAS FOR DEVELOPMENT

Collect together pictures which illustrate the Christian belief in heaven and life after death. Or invite a local minister in to talk to the group about the Christian hope in the resurrection.

**FOOTNOTES**

[1] C. S. Lewis, *The Last Battle* (Fontana Lions/Collins: London, 1950, reprinted 1980), pp 122-123,160-161,173.
[2] David Watson, *Fear No Evil* (Hodder & Stoughton: London, 1984), ISBN 0 340 34641 8, pp 170-172.

# 27

## THEME
# Personal Values

**AIM**
To consider our personal values.

**INTRODUCTION**
Show the group four photographs of yourself at different ages (eg at five, ten, fifteen, twenty years). Introduce each of your photos with a single sentence or caption to indicate where you were/ what you were doing/what was most important to you at that time (eg 'With a group of school friends on a visit to France—I wanted to see the world' etc). Use this as a springboard to talk about the way we all have values and how they change as we are growing up.

**OPTIONS AND IDEAS**

A. Give each pupil a sheet of paper with four empty picture frames drawn on it. Ask them to answer the following questions in words or pictures: (a) 'What is the most important material item you own?' (b) 'What is one belief or value you have that you would never give up?' (c) 'What three words or qualities would you give as your life's motto?' (d) 'Who or what is Number One in your life?'

B. Initiate a discussion on the different kinds of values we can have, ie material, social, personal, moral or spiritual. Ask pupils to categorise the answers they gave in section A according to the kind of values they are. Give some examples for spiritual values (ie attitudes/values in respect to a higher reality—God). Do they have any spiritual values? Explain that in the Bible Jesus talks about the importance of building life on spiritual values, eg the story about building the house on the rock in Matthew 7:24-27.

C. Get pupils to think about their personal values. Working in pairs, guide them into discussing whether or not their values have changed over the years.

D. Ask: 'If you could be someone else—who would you like to be?' Draw out the reasons for their choices and why they admire them.

E. Read the excerpts of Eric Liddell's life as told by a man who in his childhood spent more than two years in the same prison camp as Eric Liddell. Liddell was a well-known athlete whom many admired, not only for his prowess as a runner, but because he was a man who stood by his principles even when it made him unpopular and could have ended his career:

> Eric Liddell is remembered by most people as the athlete who refused to run a race on a Sunday in the 1924 Olympic Games in Paris. He later set a world record in the 400 metres, winning the gold medal. But he also became a hero to many people because of his service to God the rest of his life. Less than one year after his Olympic success, Eric Liddell

went to China as a missionary. In the late 1930s the Japanese invaded China during World War II and rounded up people they considered their enemies, including missionaries, putting them in prison camps. He was sent to Weihsien concentration camp in 1943. There Eric helped many people. His cheerful and faithful support kept people from giving up in spite of the rats, flies and disease in the crowded camp. His friendship with Jesus Christ meant everything to him. One day a week 'Uncle Eric' would look after us. His gentle face and warm smile, even as he taught us games, showed us how much he loved children. He helped organise athletic meets. I remember one story that took place in the late 1930s. As the hatred between the Japanese and Chinese grew, Eric Liddell heard about a wounded man who was dying in a run-down temple and whom none of the local people dared to help because they were afraid of the Japanese. Eric persuaded a workman to go with him with a cart to rescue the wounded man. That night in a tumbledown Chinese inn, as the two men rested on their journey, God encouraged Eric through Luke 16:10: 'He that is faithful in that which is least is faithful also in much.' The next day they reached the wounded man, lifted him onto the cart and began the journey home. As they carefully led the swaying, creaking cart along the rough road, God miraculously protected them from encircling troops. On the way, they heard of another seriously injured man. The second man had been one of six who were suspected of underground resistance and who had been lined up for beheading. Five knelt and died with one swift swish of the soldiers' swords. Because the sixth man refused to kneel, the sword missed, leaving a deep gash from the back of the man's head to his mouth. The soldiers left him to die. Villagers later came and helped him to a nearby shack. Though they were moving closer to danger, Eric and his companion went to the dying man and placed him in the cart. They walked both desperately wounded men 18 miles further to the mission hospital. Not only did this second man live, but he became a follower of Jesus Christ.

Eric died of a brain tumour just months before liberation in 1945. He was buried in the little cemetery in the Japanese part of the camp with others who had died there.[1]

Ask pupils if they admire what he did and what personal qualities Eric displayed. Ask: 'How important do you think it is to have values that you are willing to stand by?' 'What principles are important enough to you to stick with whatever happens?'

## IDEAS FOR DEVELOPMENT

Let pupils find a drawing of a real coat of arms (heraldic artists can reproduce these from recorded descriptions according to one's name). Ask pupils to design a coat of arms for themselves. Suggest they include a motto which expresses a quality they would like as a life motto (eg for truth and right).

Watch the Oscar winning film *Chariots Of Fire*.[2]

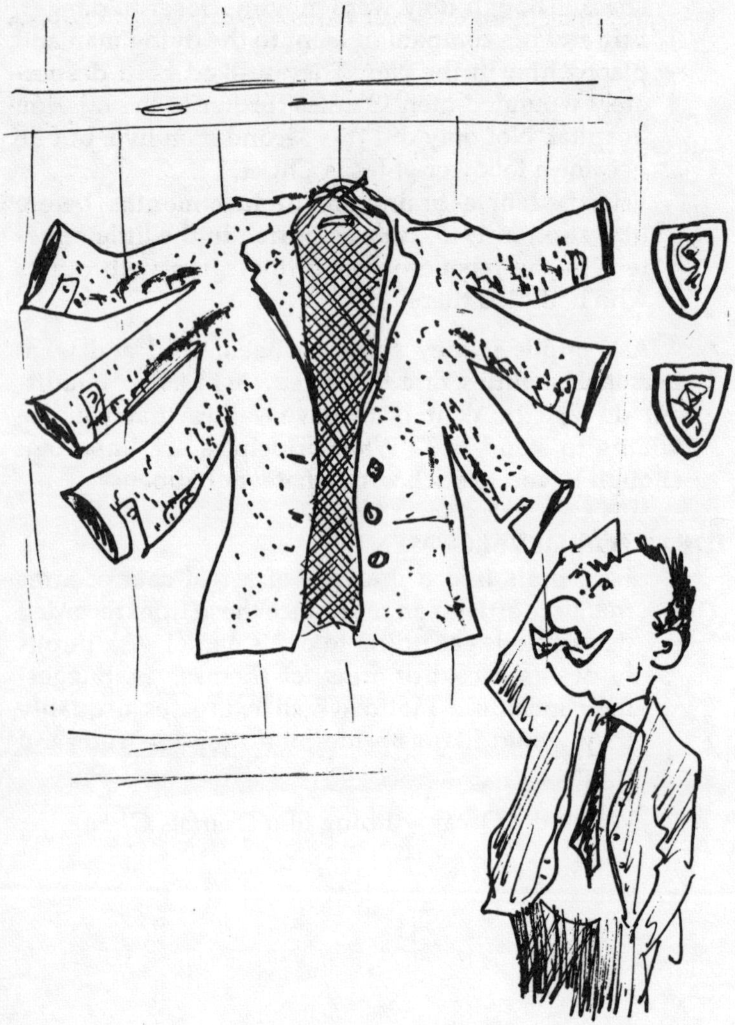

## FOOTNOTES

[1] Adapted from: David J. Michell, *I Remember Eric Liddell* (Overseas Missionary Fellowship: Toronto, undated).
David J. Michell, *A Boy's War* (OMF Books, 44 Bethel Road, Sevenoaks, Kent TN13 3UE), ISBN 9971 972 71 9. More stories about David Michell's time in a Japanese concentration camp during World War II and about Eric Liddell.

[2] *Chariots Of Fire* (CBS/Fox/Bagster Video, Westbrooke House, 76 High Street, Alton, Hants GU34 1EN, 1989). 118-minute video.

# 28

## THEME
# Language Lines

**AIM**

To show the importance of choosing the right words and to be alert to the possibility of misunderstanding.

**INTRODUCTION**

Read the extract from *Cider With Rosie* by Laurie Lee about Laurie's first day at school and how he waited all day for a present he didn't get to show how the misunderstanding of just one word caused distress to him.[1]

**OPTIONS AND IDEAS**

A. Invite pupils to share personal examples of similar types of misunderstandings of the language. Explain that words which sound the same but have different meanings are called homonyms. Give some examples:

   game—game (wild animal)
   (electric) current—current (events)—currant (raisin)

    pole—Pole (from Poland)
    forge (blacksmith's tool)—forge (a signature)
    sew (craft)—sow (farmer)—so
    two—too—to
    weight—wait
    waste—waist
    sight—site
    steak (meat)—stake (pole)

B. Point out that another barrier to understanding can be dialect. This is a variety of language, either spoken in a particular area or by a particular social group. Eg a person born and brought up within the sound of Bow Bells in East London may be referred to as a Cockney as in the TV soap *EastEnders*. Similarly, a native of Tyneside will be referred to as a Geordie like the character Spender in the TV series of the same name. Try reading this extract from *The Geordie Bible* which is based on Luke 10:38–42:

> Thor's nowt see queor as folk and nowt queoror than wimmen—speshully if the' happen te be sistors. Hev ye ivvor hord iv two that diddent quaarel? The closor the' are the mair the' fight and Mary and Martha wor nee excepshun. One minute the' wor aal ower each uthor and the next the' wor hammor and tongs. Mebbies the' did it see often cos the' liked myekin up eftor. Noo for aal the' wor sistors Mary and Martha wor as diffrent as chaalk and cheese. Martha wez the busy one. Aalwis taalkin. Aalwis workin. Nivvor sat doon. Nee mattor when ye caaled she hed hor pinny on—polishin this, polishin that; weshin this, weshin that. She aalwis smelt iv polish and carbolic. Mary wez the quiet one. She nivvor said much. She wez aalwis sittin with a byeuk in hor hand. If she wezzent readin a story she wez deein a crossword puzzle. If she wezzent deein a crossword puzzle she wez gittin

riddy for hor Sunda Schyeul Class at Bethany Chepal.[2]

C. Talk about the importance of accurate and meaningful translations if mistakes or misunderstandings are not to occur such as the following: 'When ad-men for Pepsi-Cola had their slogan "Come Alive with Pepsi" translated into mandarin Chinese, the translation turned out to mean: "Pepsi brings your ancestors back from the grave." '[3]

D. Point out that it is particularly important to be accurate when dealing with documents and manuscripts like the Bible. Draw attention to some difficulties of translating the Bible, while looking up the Bible references:

> Among the Zanaki people of Tanzania, visitors never knock on doors. They stand outside and call out their name in a loud voice then wait to be asked to come in. The only people who sometimes knock on doors are thieves who then listen to hear if anyone moves inside. If not, they think that the house is empty and go inside to see what they can steal. (Look up and read Revelation 3:20.) Someone who thinks of thieves when knocking is mentioned, would find this verse especially hard to understand. Of course, the translator put in another word meaning 'call' or 'call a greeting'.
>
> In all languages there are idioms, special ways of saying things, which would probably make no sense at all if translated a word at a time. Examples: 'White as snow', a simile used in the book of Revelation 1:14, is translated in different ways. In the Gbaya translation for the Congo it is 'white as cotton'. In Tonga (for the Pacific island with the same name) it is 'white as a flock of egrets'—large, brilliantly white birds very similar to the heron.
>
> Quechua Indians of Bolivia speak of the future as

being behind them and the past in front of them, exactly the opposite way round to our ideas. This may seem strange but it has a great deal of sense in it—after all, which can you 'see', your past or your future? Look up Philippians 3:13 to see how this difference would change the wording.[4]

Get pupils to read Mark 12:41-44 in the Authorised Version of the Bible. Let them rewrite this in simple, modern English keeping as close as they can to the meaning of the Authorised Version. Afterwards find some modern English translation like the Good News Bible, the New International Version, the New English Bible and compare the same passage with their 'translation'.

## IDEAS FOR DEVELOPMENT

Find out about the work of some organisations like the Bible Society or Wycliffe Bible Translators. Some of their publications include other examples of translation work.[5]

Do a project on Bible translators such as John Wycliffe or William Tyndale or William Cameron Townsend, the founder of Wycliffe Bible Translators.[6]

## FOOTNOTES

[1] 'Village School' in: Laurie Lee, *Cider With Rosie* (The Hogarth Press: 1959).
Laurie Lee, *The Illustrated Cider With Rosie* (Cresset Press: London, 1984), ISBN 0 7126 2913 0, p 37.
[2] Andrew Elliott, *The Geordie Bible* (Butler & Butler Publishing: Rothbury, 1986), pp 23-24.
[3] Nigel Blundell (ed), *The World's Greatest Mistakes* (Octopus Books: London, 1982), ISBN 0 7064 1128 5, p 175.
[4] Abridged from: *Bible Translation Project Book* (Bible Society: Swindon, 1989), pp 18,20.

[5] Bible Society, Stonehill Green, Westlea, Swindon, Wilts SN5 7DG, Tel: 0793-513713.

Wycliffe Bible Translators, Youth Department, Horsleys Green, High Wycombe, Bucks HP14 3XL, Tel: 0494-482521.

[6] Brian H. Edwards, *God's Outlaw—The Story Of William Tyndale And The English Bible* (Evangelical Press: Welwyn, 1976), ISBN 0 85234 253 5.

*Mary Batchelor's Everyday Book* (Lion Publishing: Tring, 1982), ISBN 0 85648 723 6, pp 16,69,128-129,133,286-289.

'God Speaks Your Language—W. Cameron Townsend' in: Elizabeth Hicks, *Living Dangerously—Stories Of Brave Christians* (Scripture Union: London, 1986), ISBN 0 86201 355 0, pp 40-50.

# 29

## THEME
# Decisions

**AIM**
  i) To think about how we make decisions.
  ii) To gain some understanding of how Christians make decisions.

**INTRODUCTION**
For the Decisions Game you will need ten pieces of coloured card, ten pieces of white card and two bowls.[1] On the white pieces of card write the type of things that people have to make decisions about. Make them a mixture of important and trivial.

Examples:
What breakfast cereal to eat.
Who will rule the country.
What job to apply for.
Where to go on holiday.
Whether to steal or not.

On the coloured pieces of card write different methods people use to make decisions.

Examples:
Toss a coin.
Refuse to decide.
Do what everyone else is doing.
Read the horoscope and decide accordingly.
Do as your parents/the school/the state says.
Pray/go by what God has said about it.
Look at the pros and cons.
Do what would cause the greatest happiness for the greatest number of people.
Vote.
Decide by committee.
Use your own conscience.

Place the two sets of cards in two separate bowls and ask volunteers to choose one from each. Each person reads out the two cards they have and say whether that would be a reasonable way of deciding in that circumstance.

Example:
What breakfast cereal to eat—pray and go by what God has said.

## OPTIONS AND IDEAS

A. Follow the game by inviting suggestions from pupils about different kinds of decisions they have to make in life. Make a note of them under the following headings: (a) decisions made on a regular basis and (b) decisions made on rare occasions. Give an example for each, eg (a) whether or not to have school dinner, (b) whether or not to end a relationship. Discuss appropriate ways to arrive at a decision on the issues raised. Share a situation of your own if appropriate and show how your decision was reached.

B. Look at the case studies below. Divide into small groups to discuss these. Appoint a chairperson to

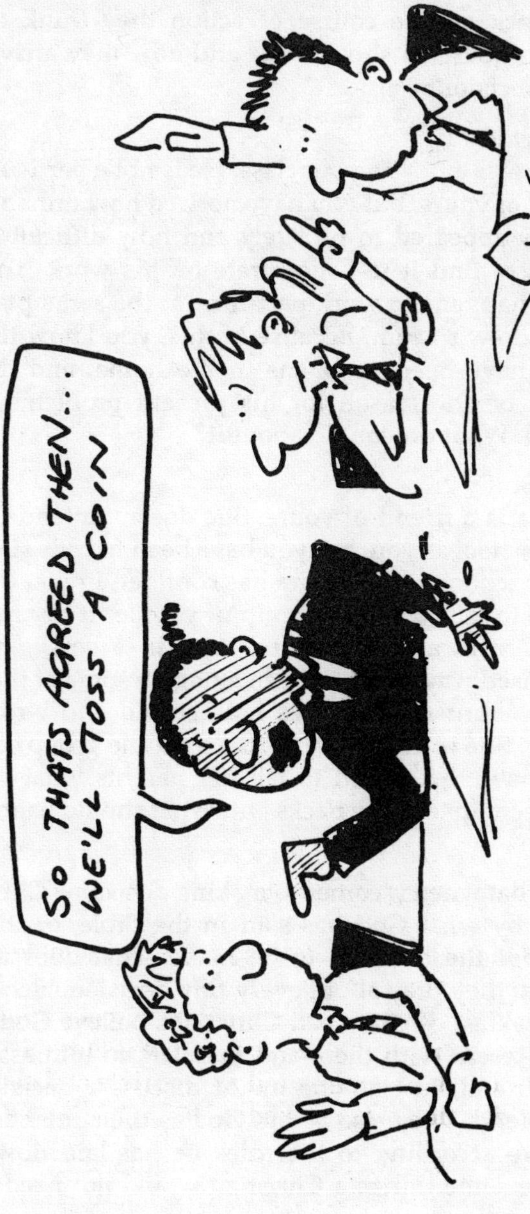
SO THATS AGREED THEN...
WE'LL TOSS A COIN

report back on the course of action they think the people in question should take and how they arrived at their decision.

Case Study 1:
Andrew is a boy in your class. He is not a particular friend of yours, but you have noticed how unhappy he has appeared to be lately and how difficult he seems to find it to concentrate on his work. Your Mum happens to work part-time at the same place as Andrew's Mum. Because of this, you know that there have been problems in the home, and this might be the reason for his present problems in school. What do you do about it?

Case Study 2:
Sandra is a friend of yours. She doesn't attend the same school as you, but you have been friends since junior school days. Sandra has confided in you that she is involved with a group of people in her new school who are into shop-lifting in a small, but organised way. She has been along on some of their 'sprees', but now realises how stupid and wrong this is. She wants to break free from the group, but they have threatened to tell her parents what she has been up to if she backs out. What should Sandra do?

C. Explain that when it comes to making decisions Christians go by what God has said in the Bible, or they pray about the decision to be made. That does not mean that they pray about every tiny decision such as what breakfast cereal to eat. Christians believe God is always present with them and they talk to him as an unseen friend, just as one might discuss a decision with a friend. They also accept God as their ruler and try to live according to the rules he has laid down. There are some things a Christian would not need to spend time over when making decisions. For example, it is quite clear in the Bible that stealing is wrong so that would be a relatively easy decision to make.

D. Here is a prayer some pupils may like to use about making decisions:

> Sometimes I think that life would be easier
> if I did not have to make so many decisions—
> if no one asked me
> which subjects I intended to study next term
> where I wanted to go on holiday next year
> what I wanted to do when I left school.
>
> Sometimes I seem to be so busy
> planning for the future
> or solving problems from the past
> that I don't have any time
> for living at this moment
> that I have now.
>
> Please God
> help me to know
> how much my yesterdays and tomorrows
> should be allowed to colour
> my today.[2]

## IDEAS FOR DEVELOPMENT

Design a simple questionnaire which sets out various problems and a range of ways of deciding what to do about each situation. Use ideas from the Decisions Game to help you. Try it out on another class, then analyse the results.

Do a project on the life of Thomas Barnado and how he changed his mind, from going to China as a missionary to opening up a children's home.[3]

## FOOTNOTES

[1] This originally appeared in: Margaret Cooling, *War And Pacifism—The Fact And The Choices* (Scripture Union: London, 1988), ISBN 0 86201 389 5, pp 12-13.

[2] Marion Stroud, *Just For You* (Lion Publishing: Tring, 1986), ISBN 0 85648 910 7, p 48.

[3] Geoffrey Hanks, *A Home For All Children* (Religious and Moral Education Press: Exeter), ISBN 0 08 024154 9.

# 30

## THEME
# Misunderstandings

**AIM**
- i) To show how a misunderstanding, incomplete information or incorrect instructions can lead to wrong conclusions or results.
- ii) To look at some examples of misunderstandings in the Bible.

**INTRODUCTION**

You will not have to live long to find out that people will misunderstand you. Tell this story to illustrate your point:

> A primary school teacher was anxious to teach her pupils the dangers of alcohol. She decided on a powerful object lesson. She filled a glass with alcohol and set it on her desk for all to see. She then put a worm into the glass and it soon died. 'What,' she asked the class, 'is the lesson taught here?' Johnny raised his hand. 'Miss,' he said, 'this teaches that if you have worms, drink whisky!'[1]

## OPTIONS AND IDEAS

A. Use the following story as an example of a misunderstanding that had a humorous outcome:

> Soon after his election, American President Calvin Coolidge invited a party of country friends to dine at the White House. Feeling rather self-conscious in such opulent surroundings, they copied Coolidge's every move. As the President poured half his coffee into his saucer, so did they. He added cream and sugar, and they did likewise. The President then laid his saucer on the floor for his cat.[2]

Point out that some misunderstandings can have far more serious results. Invite pupils to contribute personal stories about misunderstandings and their results.

B. Tell the story from the Old Testament to show how a misunderstanding nearly caused a civil war.

> The Hebrews were beginning to settle down in Israel; there were two and a half tribes on the East Bank of Jordan, and nine and a half tribes on the West Bank. The latter looked across the Jordan and saw huge piles of stones and mistakenly thought that they were raised as an altar to false gods. They began to collect a great army together to go and do battle with them—and sort them out—but before they did, they sent a delegation across to make sure what was happening. To their surprise they discovered that they weren't raising an altar to pagan gods at all, but a memorial to remind them and their children that the true real altar of God was on the other side of Jordan. A plain case of misunderstanding! (Retold from Joshua 22:1–34).

C. Explain that misunderstandings can occur because one cannot see the full picture or is not in possession of all

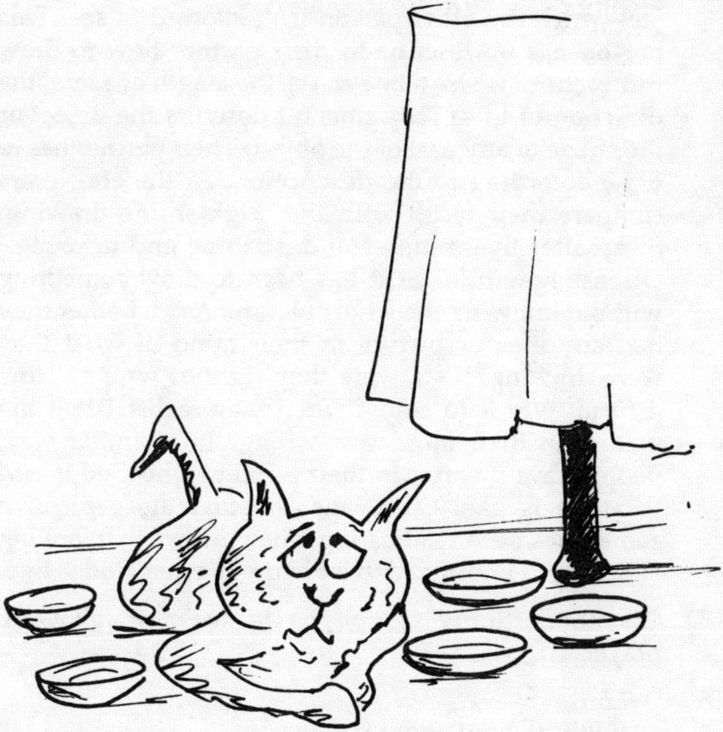

the facts. Try this game to illustrate your point. Pair pupils off and sit the partners back to back. Give one partner a line drawing (a cross, a chair, stairs, a house, etc) which the other person isn't allowed to see. This person has to describe to their partner how to draw this picture: where a line starts, the length of a line, the direction of line. They mustn't describe the object or the shape of any part of the object. Their partner has to draw according to the description. At the end, pairs compare their result with the original line drawing. Swap after five minutes of describing and drawing.[3] Discuss how difficult it has been to draw something without knowing the whole picture. Ask whether they had any idea or picture in their mind of what they were drawing. If so, were they right or wrong? How difficult was it to adjust when they realised that the picture in their mind was wrong? In a similar way, people have pictures in their mind of who God is and what he is like. Christians feel that those pictures sometimes need readjusting. They believe that looking at Jesus provides us with a picture of what God is like.

D. Give opportunity for pupils to use the following prayer:

> Lord,
> If I think hard about it,
> I don't want to live in a world of misunderstandings—I want to live in a world built on love and trust. Help me to work out any misunderstandings I have with other people and any wrong pictures I have about you.
> Amen.

## IDEAS FOR DEVELOPMENT

Ask pupils to write down some ways of avoiding misunderstandings or what to do if and when misunderstandings happen.

Find some examples from history where misunderstandings happened with serious results (eg the story of the four over-zealous knights who murdered Thomas Becket because they heard King Henry indiscreetly murmuring that he hoped someone would rid him of the Archbishop, without the King's serious intention).[4]

**FOOTNOTES**
[1] Adapted from: W. E. Thorn, *A Bit Of Honey—After-Dinner Addresses Of Inspiration, Wit And Humour* (Zondervan Publishing House: Grand Rapids/Michigan, 1964), pp 20-21.
[2] Adapted from Nigel Blundell (ed), *The World's Greatest Mistakes* (Octopus Books: London, 1980), ISBN 0 7064 1128 5, pp 82,83.
[3] John Harris-Douglas/Michael Kindred, *To Play And Pray* (CIO Publishing: London, undated), ISBN 0 7151 0386 5, pp 39-41.
[4] J. Douglas (ed), *The New International Dictionary Of The Christian Church* (Paternoster Press: Exeter, 1974), ISBN 0 85364 221 4, p 114.

# 31

## THEME

# Dead Ends

**AIM**
To think about the relevance of trusting God in situations of despair.

**INTRODUCTION**
Ask the pupils to imagine a wall in front of them. What sort of texture has the wall got? How far away from them is the wall?

**OPTIONS AND IDEAS**

A. Through movement ask pupils to explore the walls surrounding them on each side. Get them to imagine that the walls are growing bigger and coming closer. Put people into pairs to share how they felt when they were locked in this imaginary box (eg oppressed, lonely, frustrated, etc).

B. Look at the poem 'All Alone'. Then discuss different situations in which we feel 'boxed in' or trapped.

> Alone, alone
> In a wall of stone,
> All the love of the world has gone.
> Now I'm in this wall of stone.
>
> Cut off from people in this world
> All alone, all alone in this wall of stone,
> I hear the rushing of the sea,
> I wish I was not me.[1]

C. The German clergyman, Dietrich Bonhoeffer, joined the anti-Nazi pastors of the 'Confessing Church' and was imprisoned for his involvement in smuggling fourteen Jews to Switzerland. Two years later, in 1945, he was executed in the Flossenbürg concentration camp. While in prison Bonhoeffer wrote this prayer:

> O Lord God,
> great distress has come upon me;
> my cares threaten to crush me,
> and I do not know what to do.
> O God, be gracious to me and help me.
> Give me strength to bear what you send,
> and do not let fear rule over me;
> Take a father's care of my wife and children.
>
> O merciful God,
> forgive me all the sins that I have committed
> against you and against my fellow men.
> I trust in your grace
> and commit my life wholly into your hands.
> Do with me according to your will
> and as is best for me.
> Whether I live or die, I am with you,
> you, my God, are with me.
> Lord, I wait for your salvation
> and for your Kingdom.
> Amen.[2]

Suggest this prayer might be very appropriate to anyone who has been held as a hostage (eg Terry Waite, John McCarthy). Compare it with the poem above. Christians believe that Jesus is relevant to these situations because of what is written in the Old Testament about him:

> The Spirit of the Lord God is upon me, because the Lord has anointed me to bring good news to the suffering and afflicted. He has sent me to comfort the broken-hearted, to announce liberty to the captives and to open the eyes of the blind. He has sent me to tell those who mourn that the time of God's favor to them has come (Isaiah 61:1–2).

Discuss in which sense Dietrich Bonhoeffer, who was not literally released from prison, experienced a different kind of freedom through his trust in Jesus. Refer to Paul and Silas who were imprisoned because of telling people the good news of Jesus, and who were, while in prison, 'praying and singing hymns to the Lord' (Acts 16:25).

D. Ask pupils to write a poem or prayer of their own, expressing the joy of being freed/opened up when somebody breaks into their prison.

## IDEAS FOR DEVELOPMENT

Find out and write about Irina Ratushinskaya, a Christian and one of Russia's leading poets who was sentenced to twelve years in a prison camp. Her crime was 'anti-Soviet agitation in the form of poetry'. She was kept in an isolated prison cell with sub-zero temperatures. A surgeon and priest living in Birmingham pleaded, together with Amnesty International, for her release.[3]

## FOOTNOTES

[1] David Salter (nine years), 'All Alone' in: Donald Hilton (compiler), *A Word In Season—Prose And Verse For Use In Christian Education And Worship* (National Christian Educational Council: Redhill, 1984), ISBN 0 7197 0410 3, p 122.

[2] Dietrich Bonhoeffer, 'Prayers In Time Of Distress' in: *Letters And Papers From Prison* (SCM Press: London, 1971, enlarged edition), pp 142-143.

[3] Dick Rodgers, *Irina* (Lion Publishing: Tring, 1987), ISBN 0 7459 1367 9.

# 32

## THEME
# Soap

**AIM**
  i) To consider the origin and some reasons for the popularity of some 'soap operas'.
  ii) To show that God is interested in helping people cope with the real world.

**INTRODUCTION**
Ask for a show of hands to indicate who watches the various soap operas on TV. The following checklist may be helpful: *Neighbours* (BBC1), *Home and Away* (ITV), *Emmerdale Farm* (ITV), *EastEnders* (BBC1), *Coronation Street* (ITV), *The Archers* (Radio 4), *Dallas* (BBC1). Check in the Radio/TV Times or other newspaper 'guides' for some clues on what is in store in the next episode.

**OPTIONS AND IDEAS**

A. A few years ago 'soaps' meant Palmolive, Camay, Imperial Leather, etc but the origin of the phrase 'soap opera' comes from the fact that soap manufacturers sponsored long-running serial stories on radio. Today more often than not we would use this word to describe one of the above serials. Ask: 'Why do you think "soaps" are so popular?' Get pupils to explain the appeal of certain 'soaps' for them and why they find them so gripping. Suggest some reasons for the popularity of 'soaps', eg we like to see how the characters cope with situations we might face, etc. Invite other suggestions. For some people, the characters become real people whose problems actually cause some viewers to lose sleep. Some people even write in to give advice to the characters concerned!

B. Point out that Christians believe that God is permanently tuned into our lives and that he is interested in every detail of our lives—what we do, think and say. Read the following passage from the Bible to illustrate this:

> O Lord, you have examined my heart and know everything about me. You know when I sit or stand. When far away you know my every thought. You chart the path ahead of me, and tell me where to stop and rest. Every moment, you know where I am. You know what I am going to say before I even say it. You both precede and follow me, and place your hand of blessing on my head. This is too glorious, too wonderful to believe! How precious it is, Lord, to realise that you are thinking about me constantly! I can't even count how many times a day your thoughts turn towards me. And when I waken in the morning, you are still thinking of me! (Psalm 139:1–6,17–18).

C. Suggest that some people might like to use the following prayer as a way of expressing their thankfulness to God for his care and concern about us at all times. Allow a moment of quiet for this.

Dear Father God,
Thank you that you love and care for us at all times, whatever we are doing and wherever we might be. Help us to realise more each day that we can turn to you at any time of the day, that you are always there. Amen.

D. Read the poem 'The Trouble With Reality':

The trouble with reality
Is that if you miss it
There's no Omnibus Edition
To help you catch up.
The trouble with reality
Is that you can't video it
While you're out at the pub,
And fast-forward
Through the highlights
Over a hot cup of cocoa.
The trouble with reality
Is that when your friends die
They don't pop back
In the next series
To tell you
It was all a bad dream.
The trouble with reality
Is that the Casting Director
Never consults you
Before choosing
The people next door.
The trouble with reality
Is that it's easier
To watch Neighbours
Than to be one.[1]

Ask pupils for any personal instances they can recall from a soap which has played on their mind to the extent that it has preoccupied their thoughts.

E. Use the extract on the fodder factor of soaps from *User's Guide To The Media* to stimulate a debate or discussion on a controversial statement like: 'Soaps are bad for you.'

> Soap opera offers, to a society that has largely discarded religion, a fantasy in which God is almost always irrelevant. In the world of soap, people achieve happiness through their own or others' efforts. Millions of lonely, unemployed, or simply bored people watch soap endlessly. No wonder; it offers the opportunity to slip for a while into a dream world, in which such problems rarely appear.
>
> This is true of certain American and Australian (especially daytime) soaps. The British realist tradition of *Brookside* and *EastEnders* is much more open to such issues. But for millions, soap opera is a solace, a comfort, a flight from reality.
>
> But Christians believe that there really are answers to human social and spiritual needs.[2]

F. Get pupils to think about the soaps they watch and check them out against this 'Good Soap Guide':

1. *Are families portrayed as*

    a. Something to be endured?
    b. Something to be enjoyed?
    c. Something to be exploited?

2. *What is its view of the future?*

    a. The future is going to be wonderful—at least for us.
    b. If we all work hard the future could be really good.
    c. Who cares about the future when you're having fun today?

3. *What is the place of God in the soap?*

   a. Not mentioned—not really necessary.
   b. Some people seem to take him seriously but most of us aren't sure.
   c. If he really existed he wouldn't want to know us anyway.

RATING:

Three A's: This soap is probably not rotting your soul, but it's not going to turn you into a spiritual giant.

Three B's: This soap is at least in contact with real people and might make you think a bit.

Three C's: This one probably won't rot your soul either, but do you really need all that cynicism twice a week?[3]

## IDEAS FOR DEVELOPMENT

Do a survey in your school about the most popular soap operas and, using the 'Good Soap Guide', rank them accordingly.

**FOOTNOTES**

[1] 'The Trouble With Reality' in: Gerard Kelly, *Rebel Without Applause—Barbed Verse For A Comfortable World* (Minstrel/Monarch Publications: Eastbourne, 1991), ISBN 1 85424 132 X, p 116.

[2] David Porter, *User's Guide To The Media* (Inter-Varsity Press: Leicester, 1988), ISBN 0 85110 790 7, pp 30-31.

[3] *ibid* pp 34-35.

# 33

## THEME
# Letters

**AIM**
　　To think about different kinds of letters and the purposes they serve.

**INTRODUCTION**
　　Think about different types of letters (eg love letters, thank you letters, requests for payment, bills, etc). Get pupils to help by bringing in some examples from the different categories.

**OPTIONS AND IDEAS**

A. Refer to the pleasure of receiving gifts at Christmas time, and the chore of writing letters of thanks afterwards, especially if the presents were not what we really wanted! In the light of this read the following 'Christmas Thank You's':

　　Dear Auntie,

　　Oh, what a nice jumper
　　I've always adored powder blue

and fancy you thinking of
orange and pink
for the stripes,
how clever of you!

Dear Gran,

Many thanks for the hankies
Now I really can't wait for the
flu
and the daisies embroidered
in red round the 'M'
for Michael
how
thoughtful of you!

Dear Sister,

I quite understand your concern
it's a risk sending jam through the post
But I think I've pulled out
all the big bits
of glass
So it won't taste too sharp
spread on toast.[1]

B. Another important form of letter-writing is in communications between those in uniform serving their country in a time of war, and their loved ones at home. Read the extract from an actual letter written by an airman serving in the Gulf:

Sun 20 Jan 1991

Dear Mum, Dad, Anne, Emma & Kayley.
Firstly thanks very much for the letters. Glad you enjoyed your trip to Southend and I must admit I wish it had been possible to spend Xmas back in UK... Yes there is a McDonalds over here in down

town Al Khobar. The only problem is I'm on night shift at the moment so I'm not seeing much sun, but there's plenty of action...

The first three nights of the war have been tremendously exciting, a mixture of fear and euphoria: fear when the air raid red sirens sounded, and the euphoria when our aircrews returned safely from successful missions. Last night one of our aircraft returned with a bullet hole in the rudder. So far we haven't lost an aircraft but it's early days...Rest assured I'm keeping my head down and getting on with the job in hand. Who knows after this we may enter a period of longer lasting peace.... Send my love to everyone. Bye for now. Martin xxx.[2]

C. Explain that many books in the New Testament are in fact letters, the majority of which were written by Paul. The letter from Paul to an old friend of his called Philemon, a Christian businessman, is different from most of the others in that it is a personal letter about a runaway slave called Onesimus (a Greek name which means 'useful'). It seems that, contrary to his name, Onesimus had been a pretty useless slave who had run away from Philemon, but when he met Paul, he became a Christian and his life was transformed. The punishment for runaway slaves could be severe, but Paul sent 'Useful' back to his old master with a letter which you can find in the Bible called 'Philemon'. It asks Philemon to forgive Onesimus and to take him back as a Christian brother, not a runaway slave. After reading it through, ask pupils to write an imaginary reply from Philemon to Paul.

D. Several modern religious writers have used the imaginary letter as a way of communicating religious thoughts or ideas, eg *The Screwtape Letters* by C. S. Lewis. The book *From The Father's Heart* contains

I HOPE THATS NOT ONE OF THOSE CHAIN LETTERS?
SORT OF... ITS FROM PAUL, IN PRISON

imaginary letters from God. Read the following which is called 'On Your Side':[3]

> Child,
> If anyone wants you to succeed, I do. If anyone is on your side, I AM. There is no one more committed to your happiness than I, and no one even begins to love you like I do. And I want to clarify something. My love for you is more—far more—than a patronising concern for your welfare. I like you. I enjoy you. I realise you find all this hard to believe, but I want you to believe it. You'll have to sooner or later, so why not now? I think about you all the time, and I will stop at nothing to remind you of My presence. Haven't you noticed?
> Entreatingly,
> Dad

Ask pupils for their responses to this. Some might like to write a prayer in the form of a letter to God.

## IDEAS FOR DEVELOPMENT

It may be possible to arrange 'pen pals' for pupils who would like to be involved in such a scheme.

## FOOTNOTES

[1] Abridged from: Mick Gowar, 'Christmas Thank You's' in: *Swings And Roundabouts* (Collins: London, 1981), ISBN 0 00 672843 X, pp 73-74.

[2] Abridged from a letter by Sgt Martin Lonsdale dated 20th January 1991 (unpublished).

[3] Charles Slagle, 'On Your Side' in: *From The Father's Heart* (Destiny Image Publishers: Shippensburg, 1989), ISBN 0 914903 82 9, p 1.

# 34

## THEME
# It's A Mystery

**AIM**
　　i) To explore different mysteries.
　　ii) To consider some of the mysteries spoken about in the Bible.

**INTRODUCTION**
　　Prepare a 'mystery' parcel (something unusual which pupils won't guess). Start by letting one or two pupils come out and try to guess what it is. Build up the suspense! Reveal the contents of the mystery parcel at the end of the session or end of the week.

**OPTIONS AND IDEAS**

A. Use the 'Fable Of The Traveller' to show that we may never know the answer to some questions in life and there are some mysteries that we may never understand (eg questions like: Why me? Who am I? Where am I going? Is there a purpose in life?):

A traveller was walking through the night, seeing up ahead of him in the dim, rainy mist a monastery rising with the lights on. Cold and inclement was the weather, and he stopped and knocked on the door. When the abbot came, he said, 'May I come in?'

The abbot said, 'Not only may you come in, but you may eat with us.' The food was wonderful: it was warm and the monks made him very welcome. Because the weather was so bad, they asked him to stay the night. He agreed on the basis that they would supply him with a few things. 'What is it you want?' they asked.

He said, 'If I spend this night with you, I must have a room to myself, a pound of butter, a poker, a cricket bat, and a bass saxophone.' It was an unusual request, but the monks scurried around the monastery and found everything he wanted. That night the most awful progression of halftones, squeaks and squawks could be heard coming from the traveller's room. Next day, the weather continued to be bad, so the monks invited their guest to stay on. He did, but again every night he asked for that mysterious list of things: a pound of butter, a poker, a cricket bat and a bass saxophone. Each night they heard the awful noises, until finally it was time for their guest to leave. The old abbot walked him to the door and said, 'We were glad to supply all of those things, but would you mind telling me why you asked for them?'

The stranger said, 'Well, it is a family secret. It has been in our family for years and years, but if you promise not to tell another living soul, I'll tell you.' And so he told the old abbot all his heart, and the abbot, being a man of his word, never told another living soul.[1]

B. Ask if anyone has ever been on a mystery tour or a car treasure hunt. Think about the role of surprise and suspense in making these things successful. Explain that they are going to be engaged in a mystery tour around Israel in the time of Jesus. Have ready some envelopes with the clues sealed inside. Around the room should be a series of labels, each with a 'mystery place' written on it from the list below. Pupils are given the task of matching the correct clue to the right 'place'. Each clue must be numbered. Alternatively, you could prepare an outline map of Israel and indicate the places with a number instead of the name.

| CLUE | MYSTERY PLACE |
| --- | --- |
| (1) Jesus was born in this town (Luke 2:3–6). | Bethlehem |
| (2) Simon Peter and his brother Andrew used to fish on this lake (Matthew 4:18). | Galilee |
| (3) Mary and Joseph lived in this town and Jesus grew up there (Luke 2:39–40). | Nazareth |
| (4) Jesus spent forty days and nights in this area being tempted by the devil (Matthew 4:1–11). | Desert |
| (5) Lazarus and his two sisters Mary and Martha lived in this village (John 12:1–3). | Bethany |
| (6) Jesus changed some water into wine at a wedding in this place (John 2:6–11). | Cana |
| (7) Jesus brought a widow's son back to life here (Luke 7:11–15). | Nain |
| (8) Jesus wept over the evil of this city (Matthew 23:37). | Jerusalem |

C. Put pupils into groups and ask them to make a list of mystery writers, books, plays and TV series (eg Agatha Christie's *Death On The Nile*, TV film series: *Murder*,

*Mystery And Suspense*). Let them share their answers, then provoke some discussion by asking why people enjoy Agatha Christie's books, and why TV series like *Tales Of The Unexpected* were so successful (eg the element of surprise, suspense, 'could never guess who had done it').

D. The Bible talks about a special mystery which was kept secret for centuries but has now been revealed—in Jesus. Christians believe that God, who created the universe, became one of his own creatures—the man called Jesus, as Paul says in his letter to Christians at Colosse (Colossians 2:2–3).

E. Some pupils may enjoy singing or listening to the song 'Your Love For Me Is A Mystery' which expresses the mystery of God's love which never lets us down.[2]

## IDEAS FOR DEVELOPMENT

Ask pupils to find out more about some things that may be a mystery to them in that they use these things, but do not understand how they work (eg TV, computers).

## FOOTNOTES

[1] Unknown source.
[2] Rod Boreham/Dave Byrant, 'Your Love For Me Is A Mystery' in: *Songs & Hymns Of Fellowship* (Kingsway: Eastbourne, 1987), No. 639.

# 35

## THEME

# Judging By Appearance

**AIM**

To encourage pupils to think about the dangers of judging things or people just by appearance.

**INTRODUCTION**

Select three pupils to assist you in a small experiment. Have three prepared mystery packages ready and hidden from view in a bag or a bin liner. The three packages must all contain the same item (eg a chocolate bar) but each is wrapped differently: one in newspaper, one in tissue paper and one in birthday wrapping paper. They must all be the same size and weight, the only difference being the paper. Ask your assistants to draw out a mystery package from the bag. They then describe their parcel in terms of appearance, size and weight. Conduct a vote on which package most people would like to receive as a present. (The third package usually wins easily.) After the vote, the helpers open their packages in turn and reveal that each package contains the same item. Ask pupils why they voted the way they did and if they think that they ever make decisions in life like that...(ie judging something or someone by the way they look or voting for the same as their friends, etc).

## OPTIONS AND IDEAS

A. Ask who has heard the saying: 'Never judge a book by its cover'? 'What is meant by this?' 'Is it true?' Tell this Old Testament story to illustrate the point:

> The Lord said to Samuel, 'You have mourned long enough for Saul, for I have rejected him as king of Israel. Now take a vial of olive oil and go to Bethlehem and find a man named Jesse, for I have selected one of his sons to be the new king.' So Samuel did as the Lord had told him to. When he arrived at Bethlehem, the elders of the city came trembling to meet him. 'What is wrong?' they asked. 'Why have you come?' But he replied, 'All is well. I have come to sacrifice to the Lord. Purify yourselves and come with me to the sacrifice.' And he performed the purification rite on Jesse and his sons, and invited them too. When they arrived, Samuel took one look at Eliab and thought, 'Surely this is the man the Lord has chosen!' But the Lord said to Samuel, *'Don't judge by a man's face or height, for this is not the one. I don't make decisions the way you do! Men judge by outward appearance, but I look at a man's thoughts and intentions.'* Then Jesse told his son Abinadab to step forward and walk in front of Samuel. But the Lord said, 'This is not the right man either.' In the same way all seven of his sons presented themselves to Samuel and were rejected. 'The Lord has not chosen any of them,' Samuel told Jesse. 'Are these all there are?' 'Well, there is the

youngest,' Jesse replied. 'But he's out in the fields watching the sheep.' 'Send for him at once,' Samuel said, 'for we will not sit down to eat until he arrives.' So Jesse sent for him. He was a fine looking boy, ruddy-faced, and with pleasant eyes. And the Lord said, 'This is the one; anoint him.' So as David stood there among his brothers, Samuel took the olive oil he had brought and poured it upon David's head (Abridged from 1 Samuel 16:1,4–13).

Discuss the significance of the underlined passage. Ask: 'Does God judge people in the same way as we do?' Point out that if he did, David the shepherd boy might never have become one of Israel's greatest kings.

B. Put pupils into groups and give them the task of preparing a short play, a mime or a dance/drama based on the above story.

C. Read the poem 'The Dream' by Alun Haskey. Alun is a Christian and a sufferer of cerebral palsy. Despite severe physical handicap and serious speech problems (he was considered to be ineducable), he overcame this to graduate from university and now travels to share how he copes with the problem of prejudice:

> Laughed at
> Stared at
> Avoided and feared
>
> Unusual
> Astounding
> To be shunned as weird
>
> A pain
> A painful encounter
> A churning inside
> Hurried conversation
> Then run away and hide

Silently wondering who is to blame
Funny when Jesus can accept me as I am.

One day my dream will come true
Then you'll see that I'm really just like you.[1]

Ask pupils for their reaction to this poem.

D. Suggest a moment for quiet reflection when some pupils may want to ask God for his forgiveness for the times when they have made unkind or wrong judgments about people.

## IDEAS FOR DEVELOPMENT

Ask pupils to write about a person they have met who turned out to be quite different from their first impression of them.

Find out more about Alun Haskey who, being disabled, has been struggling against prejudice towards able-bodied people.[2]

**FOOTNOTES**

[1] Alun Haskey, 'The Dream' in: *Freedom Ride* (Marshall-Pickering: Basingstoke 1985), ISBN 0 551 01254 4, p 9.
[2] *ibid*
'The View From A Wheelchair' in: J. John/Sue Cavill, *Talking Heads* (Frameworks/Inter-Varsity Press: Leicester, 1990), ISBN 0 85111 211 0, pp 8-15.

# 36

## THEME

# Money/Money/Money

**AIM**
    i) To stimulate thought about the way we use our money.
    ii) To consider some Christian attitudes towards money.

**INTRODUCTION**
Show the class your prepared trick 'Two For The Price Of One'. It makes a ten pound note look like two![1]

(1) Take a £10 note, with the Queen in front of you.
(2) Fold the £10 note away from you from X to X and Z to Z.
(3) Then fold towards you the lines 'a-a' and 'b-b' (centre lines of the note).
(4) Press 'a' to the right and the corresponding fold at the back to the left and—there you have it!

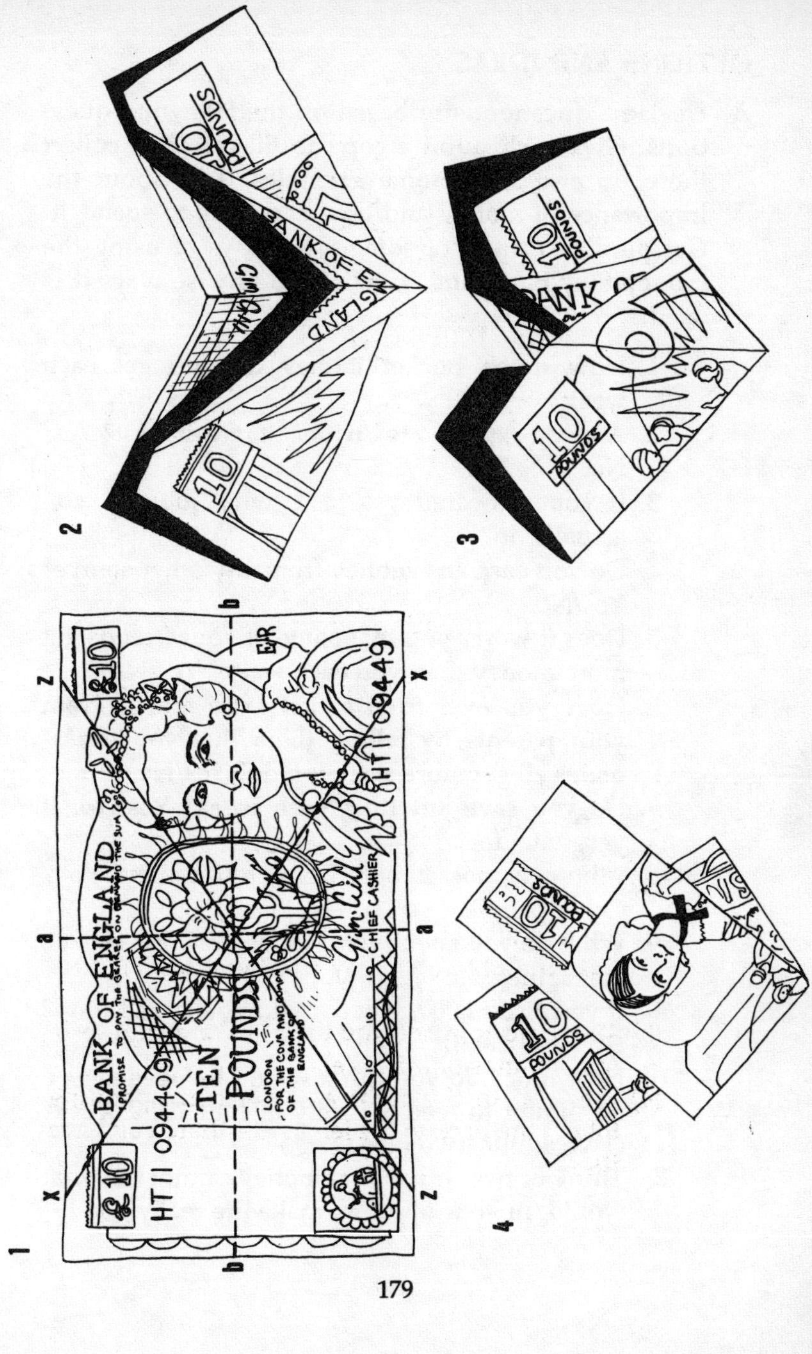
1
2
3
4
BANK OF ENGLAND
TEN
POUNDS
CHIEF CASHIER
HT11 094409
10 POUNDS

## OPTIONS AND IDEAS

A. Devise a questionnaire based on the following questions. Give each pupil a copy to fill in. Then collect these up and share some examples. Talk about the importance of money and how easy it is to spend it! Get pupils to think of some wise ways of using the money they have, and some of the unwise ways it is used.

1. How much pocket money do you get each week?
2. Are you expected to do jobs in return for it? Yes/No.
3. If you answered yes to 2, what jobs do you actually do?
4. Do you earn any money from any other source? Yes/No.
5. Does it worry you that some of your friends get more money than you each week? Yes/No.
6. Have you ever tried to get extra money from your parents by telling them that your classmates all get more than you do? Yes/No.
7. Do you save anything each week? Yes/No. If yes, what for?
8. Who gets most benefit from your money? You/Other people.
9. What do you spend your money on? Eg sweets, magazines, etc.
10. If you had £1,000, what would you spend it on? Give full details.
11. How much do you think would be needed as a minimum to feed a family of four for a week? (Two adults, two teenagers.)
12. Think of two things that money cannot buy that would, in your opinion, make life really good.[2]

B. Provoke discussion with these questions: 'Do you find it easy to give away money for fund-raising events like Children in Need?' 'Why/why not?' 'Is it easier to imagine giving away money you don't have than giving away money you do have?' 'Do you think you would really give away some of your money if you suddenly had a lot?' Suggest that what we do with the money we actually have may indicate how generous we would be if we had more of it.

C. Read the Bible passages below:

> Don't store up treasures here on earth where they can erode away or may be stolen. Store them in heaven where they will never lose their value, and are safe from thieves. If your profits are in heaven your heart will be there too. You cannot serve two masters: God and money. For you will hate one and love the other, or else the other way around (Matthew 6:19-21,24).

> Stay away from the *love* of money; be satisfied with what you have (Hebrews 13:5).

> For the *love* of money is the first step toward all kinds of sins (1 Timothy 6:10a).

Explain that Christians believe it is more important to spend time thinking about and working for things of eternal or lasting worth, than just getting all the material things we might like to have. The Bible also warns against greed (ie wanting more and more). Ask pupils to think what Jesus meant by the phrase: 'Store up for yourselves treasures in heaven.'

## IDEAS FOR DEVELOPMENT

Watch the video *Rich Man Poor Man*.[3]

Do a money survey in your own school. Devise a questionnaire which will find out how generous or mean people are.

**FOOTNOTES**

[1] 'Two For The Price Of One' in: Will Dexter, *The Illustrated Book Of Magic Tricks* (Abbey Library: London, 1957), p 110.

[2] 'Money Investigation' adapted from: Christina Lacey (ed), *JAM Magazine* January—March 1985 (Scripture Union: London, 1985), pp 42-44.

[3] *Rich Man Poor Man* (Scripture Union: London). This fifteen-minute cartoon strip, available in video or soundstrip format, is a modern parable on materialism and works well as a discussion starter on Christian values.

# 37

## THEME
# Time

**AIM**
To encourage an awareness of the brevity of life and an appreciation of the value of time.

**INTRODUCTION**
Present a large drawing on an OHP, chalkboard or large piece of card, showing several clocks indicating the time in different cities around the world (eg at London 12.00 noon GMT it will be 8 pm in Hongkong, 3 pm in Moscow, 7 am in New York, 5.30 pm in Delhi). With the help of the clocks ask the pupils to work out the time in each of these cities at 3 pm GMT in London.

**OPTIONS AND IDEAS**

A. Ask for a show of hands to indicate who owns a watch. Bring out the fact that time is important to us and shouldn't be wasted. Read Ephesians 5:16 (RSV): 'Make the most of the time because the days are evil.'

Invite suggestions about ways in which we waste time. Write these up on the board.

B. Divide the class into four groups. Ask them to work out a rough guide on how many hours a week on average they spend watching TV, at school, doing homework, sleeping, hobbies, sports, being with friends, church activities, etc. Get them to devise some way of displaying this information (eg bar chart, pie chart). Give opportunity for each group to present their findings to the rest of the class.

C. Read the quote from Mother Teresa:

> Today we have no time even to look at each other, to talk to each other, to enjoy each other, and still less to be what our children expect from us, what the husband expects from the wife, what the wife expects from the husband. And so less and less we are in touch with each other. The world is lost for want of sweetness and kindness. People are starving for love because everybody is in such a great rush.[1]

Pose the question: 'Is she right with her observation?' Provoke discussion about the quality and value of time.

D. Use an egg timer or hour glass as a visual illustration of the passing nature of time. Allow a few moments for quiet reflection on what are the really important things in life (eg things that will stand the test of time), then, working in groups, get pupils to choose one of these ideas to portray it in mime to the rest of the class.

E. Ask pupils to imagine what they would do if they discovered that the world would end in two days time. How would they plan their time? Let pupils work on this in pairs and then report back.

F.  There are times when we waste time and at other times we realise that life is short and rush around like mad. Read 'Psalm 23 For Busy People' which was written by a Japanese woman:

> The Lord is my pace-setter, I shall not rush;
> he makes me stop and rest for quiet intervals,
> he provides me with images of stillness,
> which restore my serenity.
> He leads me in the way of efficiency,
> through calmness of mind;
> and his guidance is peace.
> Even though I have a great many things to accomplish each day
> I will not fret, for his presence is here.
> His timelessness, his all-importance will keep me in balance.
> He prepares refreshment and renewal in the midst of activity,
> by anointing my mind with his oils of tranquility:
> my cup of joyous energy overflows.
> Surely harmony and effectiveness shall be the fruits of my hours
> and I shall walk in the pace of my Lord,
> and dwell in his house for ever.[2]

Pupils may like to try writing their own version of Psalm 23.

## IDEAS FOR DEVELOPMENT

Work out how old some pupils are in days, hours or minutes.

Plan a project on famous people who have given their time in the service of others, such as Sue Ryder.[3]

## FOOTNOTES

[1] Kathryn Spink (compiler), *In The Silence Of The Heart—Meditations By Mother Teresa* (SPCK: London, 1983), ISBN 0 281 04036 2, p 75.

[2] Toki Miyashina, 'Psalm 23 For Busy People' in: K. H. Strange/R. G. E. Sandbach, *Psalm 23—An Anthology* (The Saint Andrew Press: Edinburgh), p 137. (This was broadcast by Rev Eric Frost on 4th May 1965 from London.)

[3] Joan Clifford, *Faith Alive* (National Christian Education Council: Redhill, 1983), ISBN 0 7197 0385 9, pp 55-61.

# 38

## THEME
# Words/Words/Words

**AIM**

To show the power for good or bad that words can have.

**INTRODUCTION**

Ask if anyone knows the longest word in the Shorter Oxford English Dictionary.[1] The longest word is 'floccinaucinihilipilification' (twenty-nine letters). It means 'worthless'! Try pupils on some other unusual words like:

- cacography (bad handwriting or incorrect spelling—many people associate the word cacography with doctors' prescriptions!)
- tripudiation (the action of dancing or leaping; exultation).

## OPTIONS AND IDEAS

A. Talk about the power of words—select a famous speech or a piece of writing to read, such as Winston Churchill's speech on 4th June 1940.[2] Read the poem 'Words Words' by Cecily Taylor and discuss it:

> Marks on paper
> sounds in the ear
> lips shape
> words escape
> the mind grasps
> the winding tape.
> Think well the tone—
> the song by which you sing them,
> choose well, my tongue, choose well.
>
> Words chill
> drill holes
> in men's boats
> bury illusions
> confuse truth
> command death
> breathe evil
> parch interest
> shrivel hope
> dope reason—
> freezing animation
> squeezing the wounds
> building walls to keep in
> and walls to keep out.
> Think well the tone—
> the song by which you sing them,
> choose well, my tongue, choose well—
> for words can light a match
> and burn a forest down.
>
> But words thrill—
> spill tidings

>     to those who wait
>     wipe tears
>     clear boulders
>     smooth feelings
>     heal sores
>     melt distance
>     and aid love
>     remove questions—
>     flinging courage
>     ringing praises
>     praying in the silent
>     secret places.
> Think well the tone—
> the song by which you sing them,
> choose well, my tongue, choose well—
> for words can rain in drought
> and make a desert bloom.[3]

B. Make a list of important words like: yes, no, thank you, please, sorry. Discuss how some words bring pleasure and some cause hurt. Ask: 'Is this statement true: "Sticks and stones may break my bones, but words can never hurt me"?'

C. Read out these epitaphs:

> Erected to the memory of
> J MacFarlane
> Drowned in the Water of Leith
> By a few affectionate friends

> A tombstone, carved in the shape of an open book, has this inscription:
> Alfred Halstead, Book Editor
> Lent Sept 28th 1852
> Returned May 14th 1907
> (From a churchyard in Blackpool)[4]

Discuss the possible reasons behind choosing such

inscriptions and ask pupils to write some imaginary ones!

D. Encourage the pupils to think about a recent quarrel they have had. Let them make a list of phrases which are to be avoided in a conversation. For example: absolute statements such as 'You never...', 'You always...'; statements of opinion as if they were facts such as 'You are doing her an injustice', 'You can't trust him' instead of 'I feel you are doing her an injustice', 'I feel you can't trust him'.

E. David knew how easily unkind words could slip through his mouth. That is why he prayed to God to help him: 'Set a guard over my mouth, O Lord; keep watch over the door of my lips' (Psalm 141:3 NIV). Think quietly about the application which this prayer had for him and for other Christians.

## IDEAS FOR DEVELOPMENT

Search the press for interesting or funny epitaphs or look for examples of famous peoples' last recorded words and compare them.

Devise word puzzles on famous books.

## FOOTNOTES

[1] C. T. Onions (ed), *The Shorter Oxford English Dictionary* (Oxford University Press, 3rd edition: London, 1964).

[2] 'We Shall Go On To The End' in: *The Oxford Library of Words And Phrases Vol 1: The Concise Oxford Dictionary Of Quotations* (Oxford University Press/Guild Publishing: Oxford, 1981) p 71.

[3] Cecily Taylor, 'Words Words' in: John Bailey (ed), *Blueprint Book One* (Galliard/Stainer & Bell: London, 1976), ISBN 0 85249 335 5, pp 172-173.

[4] 'Dead Funny 174 & 180' in: Murray Watts, *Bats In The Belfry* (Minstrel/Monarch Publications: Eastbourne, 1989), ISBN 1 85424 008 0, pp 108,110. © Monarch Publications, used by permission.

# 39

## THEME

# Under The Influence

**AIM**
  i) To think about some of the things that influence people.
  ii) To think about the influence of the person Jesus.

**INTRODUCTION**
  Collect some advertisements, either from magazines and newspapers or from TV (in video form). Use these to trigger a short discussion on the way adverts may or may not influence people.

**OPTIONS AND IDEAS**

A. Brainstorm pupils for one minute on 'things that influence us'. Write these up as they are given (either on the board or on an OHP). Try to rank these according to their effect.

B. Examine the idea of positive and negative influences. Put pupils into groups and give them the task of designing and developing a game on this theme, eg a board game where one moves from the starting point towards the 'goal'. Progress is hampered or hastened according to two sets of 'influence cards' drawn by players. Pupils should think up positive and negative influences to write on separate cards. These would each indicate how many spaces the player should move forward or back according to the 'influence'. These would be in two separate piles and the board would indicate when either a positive or negative card has to be drawn.

C. Think about the way writers, musicians and artists can be influenced by the world around them. Give some examples: Charles Dickens whose novels often reflect the author's own background, Claude Monet who created his own water garden that featured in some of his most famous water-lily paintings, Elgar's music which is said to reflect the prosperous, opulent England of the Edwardian Era. Pupils could bring in examples of books, records or tapes which have influenced them.

D. Introduce pupils to the work of a modern composer, David Fanshawe, and play an excerpt from his work 'African Sanctus—The Lord's Prayer' to illustrate the way in which Fanshawe was influenced by African tribal music. Read pupils the composer's own account of how he got the idea for this piece:

> One day, whilst I was out fishing with a little-known tribe, the Samia, I suddenly heard, through the papyrus swamps of the lakeshore (Lake Victoria), a distant voice crying. We beached the fishing boat and waded ashore through the swamps until we broke into a clearing with a small African hut surrounded by people. They were all crying. Inside the hut I came upon the body of a dead fisherman who had died quite suddenly in the

night. At his head his mother sang, and at his feet his wife grieved. I felt uneasy producing my tape recorder but I felt it was imperative that I should record this most heart-rending song. As I stood gazing down upon the fisherman I became very moved and imagined a voice singing the Lord's Prayer.[1]

The actual lamentation for the dead fisherman translates: 'Oh, my son! Oh, what is this? Oh, my son!' Fanshawe's setting of this famous prayer and the lamentation combines African music with Western rock and ballad. Ask pupils to listen for these different influences as the music is played, and invite them to give their reactions afterwards. Invite pupils to talk about the kind of music that influences them.

E. Ask pupils to think about people who have influenced the world in which we live. Draw out suggestions, then point out that Christians have put themselves voluntarily under the influence of Jesus in their lives. Many people would also agree that Jesus has had a tremendous influence on world history (eg our calendar dates from his birth). The following article is by a Russian reviewer, who has clearly no idea who Jesus was, and who is reviewing the American film 'Jesus'.[2] If possible, show a clip from the video before you read the critique which has been translated from a Russian magazine called *Sputnik Kinorzrtelya* dated May 1991.

It is very hard to understand what is going on here, since the film contains nothing that viewers generally like to see. There are no famous actors, no spectacular chases, no striking decisions. On the contrary, the impression is given that the actors are neither 'acting' nor 'living' their roles, but rather illustrating something that they know very well. Strictly speaking, this 'something' in the film has a name—it is called 'the Gospel of Luke'. It must be assumed that this book is very well-known to all the actors, otherwise they could not appear on the screen in the manner I have described. There are unusual things in the film: its principal character appears on Earth by means of something called the 'Immaculate Conception' (which is difficult to understand, for what is immaculate about an ordinary conception? Something has obviously got lost in the translation). Then, he heals cripples by waving his hands, raises the dead, and comes back to life himself after his matter-of-fact way, as though it were the most everyday thing to bring back to life someone who had died.

The film tells the story of a man called Jesus (by the way, it is not enough to call him simply a man, so far as everyone seems to think that he is something more than an ordinary man. Not, however, in the sense of a 'superman', but in some other dimension). This is the story of a healer (not only in the physical sense) and a preacher who became aware of his destiny early in life and who, in the end, is unjustly tried and condemned to a savage execution by having his hands and feet nailed to a piece of wood in the shape of a letter 'T', which was erected like a pole.

All this is very strange, since Jesus performs exclusively good actions, protests against violence; and not only does he not corrupt the people (the crime of which he is accused) but, on the contrary, advises them not to steal, not to kill each other, and to love their neighbours, both near and far. The accusation against him that he insulted the good name of an important person called the 'Roman Caesar' and sowed dissent is also completely false. True, some of his sayings and parables do disturb both the heart and mind, but is that not the job of any teachers?

And so, on reflection, I find nothing strange in the fact that 'Jesus' has been seen by 500 million people, and I have nothing against 250 million people going to see it in our country, where hatred has hitherto had the upper hand over love.[3]

Ask pupils to consider why the influence of this one person 'Jesus' has been so great on this reviewer.

## IDEAS FOR DEVELOPMENT

Find out more about people and ideas that have influenced history or modern way of life: eg Emmeline and her daughter Christabel Pankhurst who fought for the right for women to vote.[4]

## FOOTNOTES

[1] David Fanshawe, 'The Lord's Prayer' on LP: *African Sanctus* (Philips/Phonogram: London), 6558 001.

[2] *Jesus—The Life That Changed History* (Campus Crusade for Christ/International Films, The Coach House, 55 Drayton Green, London W13 0JD). The script of this video is taken almost entirely from Luke's Gospel (Good News Version). Filmed as far as possible in authentic locations in Israel.

[3] Translated by David Ash from a Russian magazine called *Sputnik Kinorzrtelya* dated May 1991. Abridged from: *ACT NOW* Issue 26 Spring 1992.

[4] Peter & Mary Speed, *The Oxford Children's History Volume 2: The Making Of The Modern Age* (Oxford University Press: Oxford, 1983), ISBN 0 19 918187 X, pp 200-201.

## 40

**THEME**

# Pass It On

**AIM**

To consider the importance and responsibility involved in sharing information, knowledge and advice.

**INTRODUCTION**

Think up a message and play the game 'Chinese Whispers': Whisper a sentence into the next person's ear, and so on round the circle. See what it turns out like when it has completed the circuit.

**OPTIONS AND IDEAS**

A. Refer to the game to show how a message can easily become changed when it is passed on. Give the classic World War II message as an example of this: 'Send in reinforcements, we're going to advance'—which came out as 'Lend me three and four pence—I'm going to a dance!' Talk about the need for clear and accurate communication and the important consequences that can result from even one word being left out or misplaced.

B. Ask if anyone knows the 'Hot Potato' playground game.[1] Explain it: One player holds a potato or small ball. He calls another person's name and throws it to them without dropping it. How many throws before the potato is dropped, or it becomes 'cold' with dithering? Link this with the phrase 'hot potato' and explain how it is used in talking about difficult issues in politics, etc. Get the pupils to think about some current 'hot potatoes' that are in the news. Indicate how the media sometimes use such things to 'hype up' their stories. Show how people's lives and reputations can be destroyed by malicious gossip or irresponsible journalism, by finding an example from the latest news scandal, possibly about the Royal Family or other famous people.

C. Show how hurtful messages can be communicated through gossip by initiating the 'Floppy Ears And Wagging Tongues' Questionnaire:

   1. *When someone starts to tell you a bit of gossip, do you...?*

       a. Listen with all the ears you've got.
       b. Interrupt and say you are not interested.
       c. Wait till the person's finished, then ask whether they've heard what people are saying about them.
       d. Just try to ignore it.

   2. *If you've been told a piece of gossip, do you...?*

       a. Keep it to yourself—even if you know it's true.
       b. Pass it on to everyone who might be interested.
       c. Only tell one or two close friends who you can trust to keep their mouths shut.
       d. Try to find out whether it's true or not.

3. *When was the last time you passed on, or started, a piece of gossip?*

   a. Within the last 24 hours.
   b. Within the last few days.
   c. Within the last week.
   d. Can't remember.
   e. You never gossip.

4. *Think of a time when you have passed on gossip about someone. Why did you do it? Was it because...?*

   a. You didn't like the person concerned.
   b. It was great knowing something your friends hadn't heard.
   c. You knew it was true and thought other people should know.
   d. You thought it might be true and if it was, then other people should be in the picture.
   e. It was just something to talk about.
   f. You wanted to see what other people's reactions would be.

5. *If you want to keep something a secret, do you...?*

   a. Tell no one.
   b. Tell only one person, and make it clear that no one else knows.
   c. Tell more than one person, but only those you are sure you can trust.

6. *If you found out people were gossiping about you, what do you think you would be most likely to do?*

   a. Ignore it.
   b. Try to find out who started it so that you can dig up a bit of gossip about them.
   c. Go round putting the record straight.
   d. Confront those who you know have passed it on and have a go at them.[2]

Discuss the results of the questionnaire and the implications of negative talk. Refer to the Bible passages about gossip in Proverbs 18:8 and the need to control one's tongue in James 3:2b–12.

D. Talk about the way that the Christian Church has survived for 2000 years as the message of Christianity has been faithfully passed on. Think about the responsibility given to the disciples of Jesus to hand on the stories about his life and teaching. Think about the key role of people like Paul who not only travelled much to tell people the Christian message, but wrote many letters to churches (many of them from prison) in an attempt to pass on the message.

E. Ask pupils if they have received any good advice from their grandparents and if so, what it was. Get them to imagine and then write down what they, as grandparents, might pass on to their grandchildren to help prepare them for life.

## IDEAS FOR DEVELOPMENT

Talk about the use of codes and secret symbols to pass messages (eg Morse code and semaphore). Work out a 'class code' so that members of the group can communicate secret messages to one another.

Look at different types of newspapers, their style and how the same story when covered by different journalists and different styles of papers may take a different line.

Invite a missionary, who has been overseas to communicate the good news, into school to be interviewed.

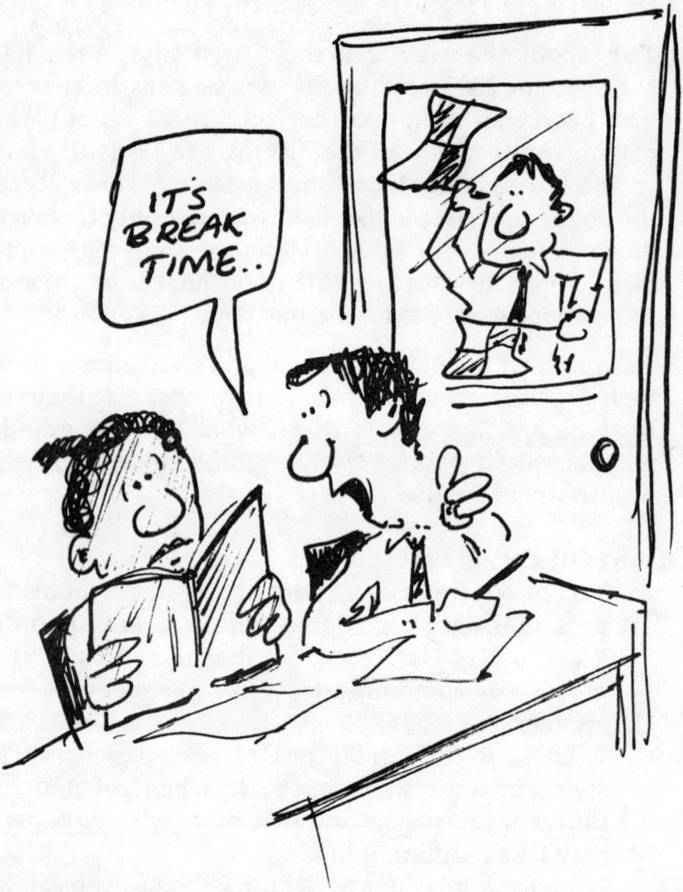
IT'S BREAK TIME..

## FOOTNOTES

[1] Pat Taylor, 'Potato Pieces' in: *The Activity Digest* Issue 4 Autumn/Winter 1989, p 17.
[2] 'Floppy Ears And Wagging Tongues' in: Christina Lacey, *JAM Magazine* August 1988 (Scripture Union: London, 1988), p 20.

# 41
### THEME
# What's Your Name?

**AIM**
- i) To think about the significance of various names and nicknames and to dissuade pupils from coining and using hurtful nicknames.
- ii) To consider the significance of some of the names of Jesus.

**INTRODUCTION**
Talk about recent interest in the meaning of certain names which may be explored through bringing in key rings, mugs, etc which carry this information.

**OPTIONS AND IDEAS**

A. Obtain a book of names and their meanings from your local public library to take into the class, and choose a few pupils names to look up. Talk about the time and care most parents take in choosing names for their children. Some pupils may be able to share how they got their names.

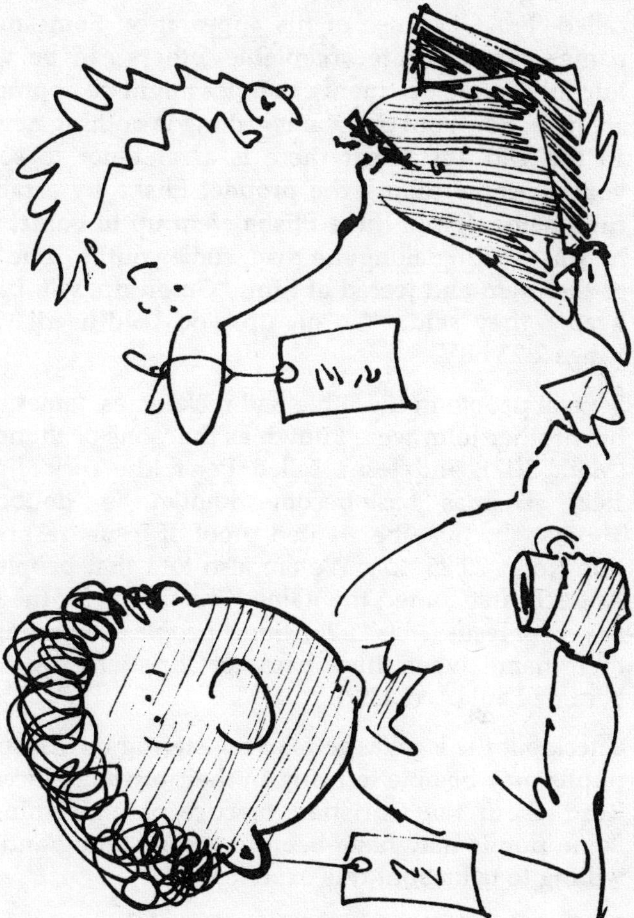

B. Talk about nicknames and their origins, eg a friend of mine was known as 'Marconi' because he was always listening to the transistor radio, another friend was called 'Frog' because of his appearance! Some nicknames can be quite acceptable, others can be very hurtful—some pertinent examples might be appropriate here. Point out that name-calling is nothing new—in the Old Testament there is a reference to some young people calling the prophet Elisha by a rather rude name: 'From there Elisha went up to Bethel. As he was walking along the road, some youths came out of the town and jeered at him, "Go on up, you bald-head!" they said. "Go on up, you bald-head!" ' (2 Kings 2:23 NIV).

C. Several people in the Bible had nicknames. James and his brother John were known as the 'sons of thunder' (Mark 3:17), and Jesus called Peter 'the rock' (John 1:42). Thomas has become known as 'doubting Thomas' because he wanted proof of Jesus' resurrection (John 20:25–27). We are also told that people at Antioch first coined the name 'Christians' for the followers of Jesus (Acts 11:26). Some people even changed their name when they became Christians, eg Saul became Paul (Acts 13:9).

D. Check out the legal aspects of registering births, some pupils may be able to bring in their birth certificates. Read about the Christian practice of christenings.[1] Some pupils may have been to a christening and be willing to talk about this experience.

E. Look at the origins of names, such as 'Johnson', which is derived from 'son of John'. In Scotland and Ireland 'Mac' or 'Mc' mean 'son of' (eg 'MacDonald' means 'son of Donald'). This also exists in other languages. Here are some examples: in German the word 'sohn' is often tagged at the end of a name, so 'Mendelsohn' means 'son of Mendel', in Aramaic 'Bar-Abbas' means 'son of Abbas', in Arabic, 'Ibn' has the meaning 'son'.[2]

Read this prayer from a Hebrew Hasidim (ie somebody who belongs to the ultra-orthodox wing of Judaism): 'Grant us, O Lord, that we may never forget that every man is the son of a King.'[3]

F. Many different names and titles are given to Jesus in the Bible. Either look these up and ask pupils to write a brief explanation of what each title or name conveys about God's character or, alternatively, invite suitable individuals from local churches to explain the significance of a name or title and what it means to them personally. Here are a few to try:

Light of the World (John 8:12).
King of kings (1 Timothy 6:15).
Good Shepherd (John 10:11).
Bread of Life (John 6:35).
Prince of Peace (Isaiah 9:6).
Son of David (Matthew 1:1).
Lord of all (Acts 10:36).

G. When Jimmy Savile was asked for his favourite 'Bible Bit' he quoted the passage in Isaiah 9:2,6–7.[4] This contains many titles and names which refer to the Son of God (Jesus) and is often read in carol services. Give opportunity for pupils to reflect on this passage by reading it aloud with a piece of suitable Christmas music playing softly in the background.[5]

## IDEAS FOR DEVELOPMENT

Find out about different naming ceremonies and any religious practices associated with these.[6]

Many surnames are derived from nicknames, eg Redhead, places or geographical names, eg Hill, or occupations, eg Smith. Pupils may enjoy finding out about their own surnames.

## FOOTNOTES

[1] Kevin O'Donnell, *From The Cradle To The Grave* (Edward Arnold/Hodder & Stoughton: Sevenoaks, 1987), ISBN 0 7131 7591 5, p 22.
David Self, *Living A Faith* (Macmillan Education: Basingstoke, 1987), ISBN 0 333 39218 3, pp 4-9.

[2] ibid, p 6.

[3] 'Hebrew Hasidim' in: John Carden, *Another Day—Prayers Of The Human Family* (Triangle/SPCK: London, 1986), ISBN 0 281 04251 9, p 68.

[4] Janet Green, *Best Bible Bits* (CIO Publishing: London, 1984), ISBN 0 7151 0420 9, p 31.

[5] Fletch Wiley, *Repeat The Sounding Joy!* (Word UK Music: Milton Keynes, 1990). Cassette/CD with Fletch Wiley playing Christmas carols on the trumpet.

[6] O'Donnell, *op cit*, pp 16-24.
Christine Brittain/Michael Tredinnick, *Landmarks In Life Books 1 & 2* (Blackie & Son: Glasgow, 1986), ISBN 0 216 91845 6/0 216 92365 4.

# 42

## THEME

# You Are Unique

**AIM**

To emphasise human uniqueness and show how everything we do bears our mark.

**INTRODUCTION**

Have ready some thumbprints from staff or a few pupils. Use non-toxic ink and make two thumb-prints from the same person! Photocopy a class set, and investigate them (ie their different sizes, designs and patterns).

**OPTIONS AND IDEAS**

A. Ask pupils to play detectives and to find the two thumb prints which are by the same person (same thumb!).

B. Read the poem 'Thumbprint' by Eve Merriam:

In the heel of my thumb
are whorls, whirls, wheels
in a unique design:

mine alone.
What a treasure to own!
My own flesh, my own feelings.
No other, however grand or base,
can ever contain the same.
My signature,
thumbing the pages of my time.
My universe key,
my singularity.
Impress, implant,
I am myself,
of all my atom parts I am the sum.
And out of my blood and my brain
I make my own interior weather,
my own sun and rain.
Imprint my mark upon the world,
whatever I shall become.[1]

C. Talk about how unique our fingerprints are, even in identical twins. Christians believe that not only are our fingerprints unique, but that each person is a 'one off'. Read Psalm 139:13–14:

> You made all the delicate inner parts of my body, and knit them together in my mother's womb. Thank you for making me so wonderfully complex! It's amazing to think about. Your workmanship is marvellous—how well I know it.

It doesn't talk about fingerprints but needlework!

D. If possible, invite a local police officer in. Ask how the police use fingerprints to identify wanted persons. The owner of a house or a shop makes fingerprints all over the place, they are called legal fingerprints. The police then try to find fingerprints which are different and match them up with fingerprints from people who are in their files. We mark everything we touch. Write a list of all the objects you have touched during one day.

If your fingerprints were easily visible or even coloured, where would they be seen? Ask: 'Would this have any effect on you?' 'What would this reveal about yourself?'

E. Christians believe that everyone leaves a special mark not only on things, but also on people and events (ie everyone makes a difference to the classes they attend, the games they share, the friends they make). We leave our mark on the world. Give pupils some minutes of quiet reflection on how they can make a difference in their friendships, in their work at school, in relationships with their family, in their spare time.

F. Get into pairs. One person pretends to be the sculptor, the other person the 'clay'. The sculptor then moulds the other person into a shape or position of their choosing (eg a mood or a special characteristic of the 'clay' person). The 'model' 'freezes' in this position so that other members of the group can look at them. The model and the sculptor then swap roles. This activity explores human moulding and modelling and illustrates that we shape each other through our relationships.

## IDEAS FOR DEVELOPMENT

Ask pupils to bring along items, they themselves, their parents or grandparents have made (embroidery, knitting, sewing, crocheting).

Explore different patterns and designs.

Study the life of people who influenced their environment or society towards more peace and justice (eg the prison reformer Elizabeth Fry, Martin Luther King or Benjamin Waugh, the founder of the NSPCC).[2]

## FOOTNOTES

[1] Eve Merriam, 'Thumbprint' in: Patricia McCall/Sue Palmer, *Presenting Poetry 3* (Oliver Boyd: Edinburgh, 1986), ISBN 0 05 003727 7, p 24. Originally from: Eve Merriam *A Sky Full Of Poems* (© 1964, 1970, 1973) Reprinted by permission of Marian Keines for the author.

[2] Catherine Swift, *Elizabeth Fry—Friend Of Prisoners* (Marshall Pickering: Basingstoke, 1986), ISBN 0 551 01355 9.

Mary Drewery, *Martin Luther King* (Marshall Pickering: Basingstoke, 1984), ISBN 0 551 01104 1.

R. J. and J. Owen, *NSPCC* (Religious and Moral Education Press: Exeter, 1987), ISBN 0 08 034379 1.

# 43

## THEME

# Why Me?

**AIM**

i) To think about some of the tragic things that happen to people.
ii) To consider the role of personal faith in coping with problems.

**INTRODUCTION**

Have a number of pictures that show various forms of suffering in the world (eg a battered or neglected child, a leper, a handicapped person, an earthquake victim, a victim of a violent crime). Suggest that all these people might ask the same question: 'Why me?'

**OPTIONS AND IDEAS**

A. Point out that most of us don't have to try to cope with these terrible situations or huge problems, but on a more mundane level, most of us have problems and 'disasters' of some kind or another (eg Adrian Mole's problem with his nose!).[1] Allow two minutes for

211

pupils to get into pairs and discuss an occasion when they said or felt like saying 'Why me? Why did this have to happen to me?' Ask for examples if appropriate.

B. Point out that many people, even when they have a strong Christian faith, sometimes still ask the question: 'Why me?' Talk about these famous characters from Old Testament stories who thought this way on at least one occasion:

> *Job* lost his sons and daughters, his servants and his wealth in a series of disasters on one single day. He also got painful sores from the soles of his feet to the top of his head (Job 1—2). When all that happened to him he came close to despair and said: 'Why didn't I die at birth?' (Job 3:11).
>
> *Gideon* expressed the thought that God had let his people down: 'If the Lord is with us, why has all this happened to us? And where are all his miracles our ancestors have told us about—such as when God brought them out of Egypt? Now the Lord has thrown us away and has let the Midianites ruin us' (Judges 6:13).

C. Sometimes people appear to suffer through no fault of their own. At other times it is obvious it is something we bring on ourselves. Ask for examples of both. Discuss some of the problems associated with suffering (eg difficulties with getting out if you are in a wheelchair, people talking about you, feeling sorry for yourself).

D. Read Adrian Plass' poem 'My Baby'. He struggled with the question of why God let King David's baby boy die. This baby was the result of David's adulterous relationship with Bathsheba, who was already married to a soldier called Uriah. David sent Uriah to the front line so that he would die and Bathsheba would be free to marry him. Explore the perspective from which this poem was written:

> I wish you knew how much I love you all. I wish you could trust me in the way that David did. You've asked me a question about the death of a baby. Now I will ask you some questions, and you must decide whether I have earned the right to be trusted whatever I do. My questions are about Jesus.
>
> When he was dragged from the garden of Gethsemane after a night of agonised prayer and terrible, lonely fear; when he was put on trial simply for being himself, and beaten, and kicked, and jeered at; did I insist that you solve for me the problem of pain? I let you hurt and abuse my son—my baby.
>
> When he hauled himself, bruised and bleeding along the road to his own death, knowing that a single word from him would be enough to make me release him from his burden, did I let you down? No, I let you crush him under the weight of your cross. My son—my baby.
>
> And when the first nail smashed into the palm of his hand, and everything in my father's heart wanted to say to those legions of weeping angels, 'Go! Fight your way through and rescue him. Bring him back where he belongs', did I abandon you to judgment? No, I let you kill my son—my baby.
>
> And when he had been up on that accursed cross for three long hours, and with every ounce of strength left in his poor suffering body, he screamed at me, 'Why have you forsaken me?' did I scream back, 'I haven't! I haven't! It's all just a nightmare—come back, they aren't worth it!'

No, I loved you too much—far too much to do that. I let your sin cut me off from my son—my baby.

And that death, dismal, depressing and horribly unjust as it was—the death of my innocent son, has brought peace and life to millions who've followed that same Jesus, who came back to life, back to his friends, and back to me.

Trust me. When it comes to the death of babies— believe me—I do know what I'm doing.[2]

## IDEAS FOR DEVELOPMENT

Find out about 'Joni' who broke her neck in a swimming accident and is now paralysed and confined to a life in a wheelchair. Read about her struggle to come to terms with this or watch the video.[3]

## FOOTNOTES

[1] Sue Townsend, *The Growing Pains Of Adrian Mole* (Methuen: London, 1984), ISBN 0 7493 0222 4, pp 13-14. Diary entries from April 4th and 5th.

[2] 'My Baby' in: Adrian Plass, *Clearing Away The Rubbish* (Minstrel/Monarch: Eastbourne, 1988), ISBN 1 85424 025 0, pp 95-96. © Monarch Publications, used by permission.

[3] Joni Eareckson, *Joni* (Pickering & Inglis: Glasgow, 1976), ISBN 0 7208 0412 4.
*Joni* (Worldwide Films/Bagster Video, Westbrooke House, 76 High Street, Alton, Hants GU34 1EN). Video: starring Joni Eareckson as herself.

# 44

## THEME

# I Believe

**AIM**

To provoke thought about the importance of belief in God in relation to prayer.

**INTRODUCTION**

Conduct a class poll on: 'When do you think most people pray?' Draw a simple chart on the board or OHP to list ideas and add other ideas to your list:

| People Pray When: | Votes |
|---|---|
| They or someone close to them is ill. | |
| Facing a difficult test or exam. | |
| They are trying to 'kick' a bad habit. | |
| They are afraid. | |

## OPTIONS AND IDEAS

A. Ask: 'Where do people seek help?' Talk about the fact that many young people have a lucky mascot they take into the exam room or on to a quiz show with them. Ask pupils: 'Why do they do this?' 'Can mascots really help them do well?' 'Why/why not?'

B. Invite two pupils who have already been prepared to read or act out this conversation about facing an exam. Wait for pupils' reaction to this sketch:

Two people hold the following conversation about forthcoming exams. B has a bag of goodies.

A: Well, how are you feeling about the exam? Nervous? You look it. Have you got everything you'll need for the exam. Let's have a look. (Unpacks bag and holds them up for all to see). Pen and refill—and Tipp-Ex—very good. Polos—yes; Kleenex—yes; deodorant—well er...; Teddy bear!—Teddy bear? Why have you brought this?

B: For good luck. It's a mascot. It helps me!

A: What! Are you saying that because Teddy bear will be sitting on your desk, that somehow the questions will only be the ones you can answer—despite the efforts of the examiner who prepared the questions four months ago?

B: Well, er...

A: Or will you whisper to Teddy and ask him to tell you the answers?

B: Well...

A: What's it like praying to Teddy? I never realised an eighteen inch bright yellow furry creature with pink bow, one eye missing and a stomach full of straw had such divine powers!!

B: Well...Don't you pray?

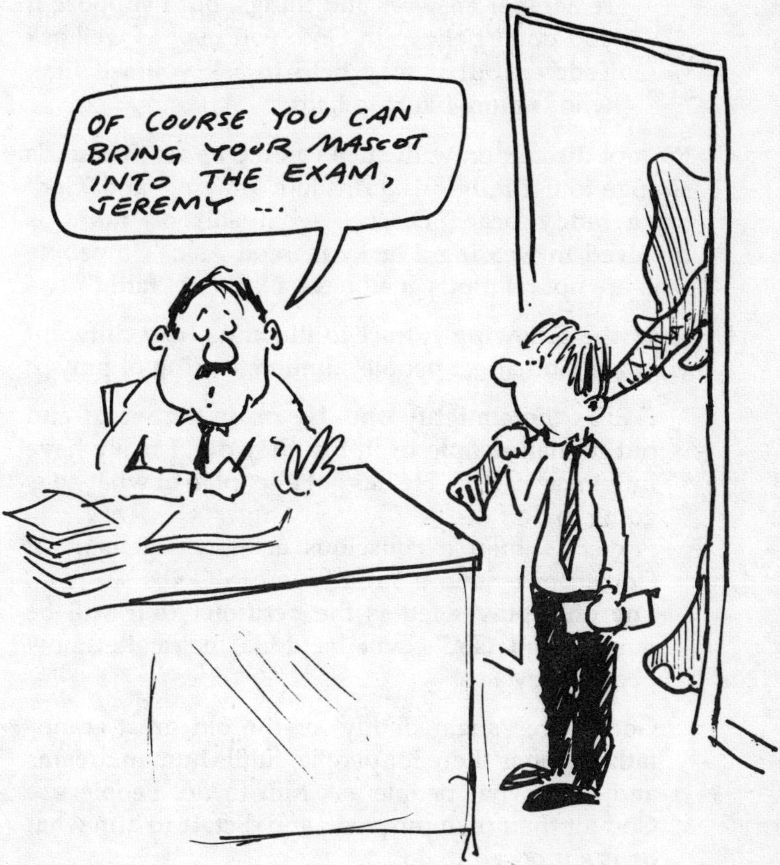
OF COURSE YOU CAN BRING YOUR MASCOT INTO THE EXAM, JEREMY ...

A: I think it's reasonable to pray. Someone probably can help—and that's what God is about. I mean if God is God then obviously God's got an idea about me and may be able to help me remember answers and things. But I suppose if you don't believe in God, you may as well ask Teddy...but it may help to ask yourself first, who is more likely to help.

C. Prompt discussion with such comments as: 'It sounds strange to use religious terms like 'praying' and 'God' for a teddy bear!' Discuss what sort of 'faith' is involved in wearing a lucky mascot. Ask: 'Do people who are not religious at all have a kind of "faith"?'

D. Read the following extract to illustrate how different views of God affect people's understanding of prayer.

> God is the almighty one. He made the world and put human people in it, but they don't really have influence on him. He has got a set plan of what he is going to do.
> Prayer is then a conscious acknowledgement of God's power and a submission to God's set plan. The only prayer left is the petition 'Your will be done'—and God's will be done, no matter how people pray.
>
> God is the 'sugar daddy' or the old great-grandfather who is there for people, fulfils human dreams and does what people ask him to do. People use God for their own purposes and dictate to him what he is supposed to do.
> Prayer is then an attempt to manipulate God. God becomes like a sweets' slot-machine in which people insert their prayers and out of which come the answers from God.
>
> God is either bound to a cause-and-effect universe

and hasn't got the power to do anything else apart from what is 'natural' in this world anyway. That means he cannot or does not interfere with this world, or a bit of God is in everything, in every person and in every thing.

Prayer does not make sense very much, because God (similar to the mascot) is powerless and is not a real conversation partner. Prayer is then a monologue which might have some positive therapeutic effect.[1]

Ask pupils to write on a piece of paper what they mean by 'God' and 'prayer'. Stress that their comments can be anonymous. Collect in the pieces of paper and read out some of their answers. Ask pupils to help you put together some ideas on what God is like based on what they know about Jesus from the New Testament writings.

## IDEAS FOR DEVELOPMENT

Conduct a survey amongst other pupils. Some of the questions could be: 'Do you believe in God?' 'If yes, what sort of God do you believe in?' 'If no, why/why not?' 'What do you think happens after this life?'

Find out what other religions believe about what God is like.[2]

## FOOTNOTES

[1] Adapted from: *Our World Belongs To God—A Contemporary Testimony*—Study Version (CRC Publications: Grand Rapids/Michigan, 1987), p 34.Used by permission.

[2] Linda Smith, *All About Living 1* (Lion Publishing: Tring, 1986), ISBN 0 7459 1160 9, pp 23-24.
Kevin O'Donnell, *Godtalk—Themes And Questions In World Religion* (Collins Liturgical Publications: London, 1986), ISBN 0 00 599803 4, pp 39-56.
Robert Kirkwood, *Looking For God* (Longman: Harlow, 1987), ISBN 0 582 20255 8.

# 45

**THEME**

# Coping With Death

**SPECIAL NOTE:** THIS MATERIAL HAS BEEN PREPARED TO ASSIST TEACHERS FACED WITH BEREAVEMENT WITHIN THE SCHOOL CONTEXT. IT IS NOT INTENDED FOR GENERAL USE.

## AIM

To find some acceptable ways of helping pupils in handling the experience of losing a pupil or a member of staff they knew and loved.

## INTRODUCTION

Have two different types of textbooks to show pupils. One with answers in the back, and one without. Use these to illustrate the point that sometimes there are no built-in answers to life's puzzles and problems. Some things remain a mystery all our lives.

## OPTIONS AND IDEAS

A. Accompany the lighting of a candle with the words of Proverbs 20:27 (AV): 'The spirit of man is the candle of the Lord, searching all the inward parts.'

B. The talents of Joyce Grenfell and her ability to entertain in her unique way may be known to some. She penned the following verse which could be read:

> If I should go before the rest of you,
> Break not a flower nor inscribe a stone.
> Nor when I'm gone speak in a Sunday voice,
> But be the usual selves that I have known.
> Weep if you must,
> Parting is hell,
> But life goes on,
> So sing as well.[1]

C. To sing, as the above verse says, is not easy at times of real grief. For many years, the singer and harpist Mary O'Hara, herself a friend of Joyce Grenfell, lost her desire to bring pleasure to those who admired and loved her music-making with the tragic death of her young husband, Richard Selig, after just fifteen months of marriage. Allow pupils to silently read Michael O'Leary's account of the final moments of Richard's life reproduced from the book *The Scent Of The Roses*.[2]

D. Explain that the title *The Scent Of The Roses* was taken from a song based on a poem written by Thomas Moore, which Mary O'Hara was writing a harp accompaniment for during the time her husband was dying. Listen to a recording of this song if possible, paying particular attention to the last four lines:

> Long, long be my heart with such memories filled
> As the vase in which roses have once been distilled.
> You may break, you may shatter the vase if you will,
> But the scent of the roses will hang round it still.[3]

Think about the idea behind these words.

E. Read the story 'The Legend Of The Raindrop':

The legend of the raindrop
has a lesson for us all
As it trembled in the heavens
questioning whether it should fall—
For the glistening raindrop argued
to the genie of the sky,
'I am beautiful and lovely
as I sparkle here on high,
And hanging here I will become
part of the rainbow's hue
and I'll shimmer like a diamond
for all the world to view'...
But the genie told the raindrop,
'Do not hesitate to go,
For you will be more beautiful
if you fall to earth below,
For you will sink into the soil
and be lost a while from sight,
But when you reappear on earth,
you'll be looked on with delight;
For you will be the raindrop
that quenched the thirsty ground
And helped the lovely flowers
to blossom all around,
And in your resurrection
you'll appear in queenly clothes
With the beauty of the lily
and the fragrance of the rose;
Then, when you wilt and wither,
you'll become part of the earth
And make the soil more fertile
and give new flowers birth'...
For there is nothing ever lost
or eternally neglected
For everything God ever made
is always resurrected;[4]

F.  Invite any member of the group who so wishes, to join silently in the following prayer:

> Lord, today we have joined together to remember _____ with affection and gratitude. We thank you for the fragrance of _____'s life that remains with us in the form of happy memories and past joys. We pray for all members of the family who will miss _____'s presence in the home, we pray for close friends who will miss _____ company at school and at play. Help us to remember that after the darkness of winter, spring comes, breathing new life in everything, and all the flowers that fell in death will eventually be awakened by the breath of spring. This we ask in your name. Amen.

Note: This prayer may be adapted to include some of the pupil's positive characteristics.

## IDEAS FOR DEVELOPMENT

This is obviously not a subject to be developed in the usual way, but pupils may wish to club together to purchase a shrub or rosebush for planting in a suitable place in the school grounds.

**FOOTNOTES**

[1] Joyce Grenfell, 'If I Should Go Before The Rest Of You' from: *In Pleasant Places* (Macmillan & Futura: London). © The Joyce Grenfell Memorial Trust 1989. Reproduced in: Mary O'Hara, *Celebration Of Love* (Hodder & Stoughton: London, 1985), ISBN 0 340 37323 7, p 158.

[2] Mary O'Hara, *The Scent Of Roses* (Fontana/Collins: Glasgow, 1980), pp 182-183.

[3] Thomas Moore, *Farewell But Whenever* quoted in: ibid pp 176-177. Mary O'Hara, 'The Scent Of The Roses' On cassette tape: *The Scent Of The Roses* (Chrysalis Records: 1980), ZCHR 1308.

[4] Helen Steiner Rice, *Someone Cares—The Collected Poems Of Helen Steiner Rice* (Fleming H. Revell Company: Burlington, 1972), p 108. Used with permission of Helen Steiner Rice Foundation.

# 46

## THEME
# Harvest

**AIM**
To encourage pupils to think about the unfairness of the way the world's harvest is divided and how it might be shared out more fairly.

**INTRODUCTION**
Ask pupils to imagine it is their birthday and as a special treat they can choose all their favourite foods for a birthday meal. What would they have? Get them to write down their special menu.

**OPTIONS AND IDEAS**

A. Select a few children to read out their menus. Compare their meal with the staple diet of the Miskito Indian which consists of rice and beans. If you have time you may like to recreate this special Honduran meal as a birthday treat:

> The staple diet of the Miskito Indians is rice and beans. On special occasions they add cheese and eat

it from a fondue-style pot with tortillas and bread. Boil some rice (2 ounces of uncooked rice per person). Use some tinned cooked red kidney beans (1 tin to 3 or 4 people). Either serve this with the rice and put the cheese on top (any type will do—the most authentic would be low-fat soft cheese) or put the beans in a fondue pot and add the grated cheese while the beans keep hot over the spirit burner or on a hot plate. Tortilla crisps can be bought in supermarkets, and pitta bread is pretty close to the Honduran original. It's a great meal, and healthy too![1]

B. Play this 'World Food Cupboard Game':

*Preparation:* Find a list to show GNP (Gross National Product) for the countries of the world. A good atlas or library should produce this.[2]
Select 6 bands of countries based on GNP:
  (1) the most wealthy = cake
  (2) the next most wealthy = 1 roll
  (3) the next band = ½ roll
  (4) the next band = ¼ roll
  (5) the next band = ⅛ roll
  (6) the next band = a bag of crumbs

Select the names of three countries from each band and write them on cards. Under the country's name write what they receive from the world food cupboard, ie:

| Switzerland<br>Cake | UK<br>1 roll | USSR<br>½ roll |
| --- | --- | --- |
| Brazil<br>¼ roll | Indonesia<br>⅛ roll | Bangladesh<br>crumbs |

Having completed three cards from each band (eighteen in all), make a second set of cards with the names of eighteen pupils on the cards. (Make sure that the pupils chosen will not be intimidated by coming out to the front.) Set up a world food cupboard at the front of the room. In it there will be 3 slices of cake, 3 whole rolls, 3 x ½ rolls, 3 x ¼ rolls, 3 x ⅛ rolls, 3 bags of crumbs.

Have a lucky dip bag and a bag to draw pupils' names from.

*How To Play The Game:* Ask the first person to come and choose a country to be born into. Then give that person a slice of cake, a roll, a bit of a roll or a bag of crumbs—whatever is appropriate to the GNP of this country. Repeat this with the rest of the eighteen pupils.

*Comment:* Don't forget to collect scraps of bread so that the caretaker doesn't have to tidy up after you!

Explain that although this is a game, there is a serious message behind it. Ask some children afterwards to describe how they felt when they received the bread, the cake or the crumbs. Ask: 'Was it fair?' 'Was there a reason why you got the crumbs, cake, etc?' Explain that this is how the world's food is shared. Contrast the truth that thousands of people are starving with the fact that lots of people in the West are on diets trying to lose weight.

C. Have some food adverts ready to show to the group. Ask them to suggest how the advertisers have tried to make their products appealing.

D. Compile a list of ways in which you could help in sharing all that we have in the 'First World' with people suffering from malnutrition and famine in the Third World. Here are a few ideas to help:

—I can waste less generally (water/food/clothes/

money, etc) and try to recycle as many items as possible to cut down on the use of the earth's resources.

— I could join a group which studies problems of world development and which organises campaigns, exhibitions, concerts, fasts, sponsored walks, street theatre, handing out leaflets and putting pressure on politicians.

— I will pray regularly for the Third World and for the poor and distressed people who appear on the TV screen.

— I could buy my Christmas and birthday presents from Tearcraft or Traidcraft and in this way help Third World producers to provide employment and income.

— I could sponsor a child or a trainee who could then get a better education and find work.

— As a class we could collect 10p pieces in old loo rolls for an agency like Tear Fund.

— When I am old enough, I could share my skills for some time and work for an organisation which is doing something to reduce world poverty.[3]

Select one or two of the best ideas for sharing our resources and challenge pupils to commit themselves to do something on a long-term basis.

E. The following prayer written by an African Christian may be appropriate:

> I saw a child today, Lord, who will not die tonight, harried into hunger's grave. He was bright and full of life because his father has a job and feeds him, but somewhere, everywhere, 10,000 life-lamps will go out, and not be lit again tomorrow. Lord, teach me my sin. Amen.[4]

**IDEAS FOR DEVELOPMENT**
Compare diets from around the world. Work out how many calories there would be in each meal.

**FOOTNOTES**
[1] 'A Honduran Harvest Supper' abridged from: Tear Fund, *Third Track* Issue 4 July 1990, p 12.
[2] Geoffrey Barraclough (ed), *The Times Concise Atlas Of World History* (Times Books: London, 2nd edition, 1986), pp 150-151.
[3] Adapted from: *Tear Fund—A Resource Pack For Secondary Schools* (Tear Fund: Teddington, undated).
[4] Ron Ingamells (ed), *Windows Into Worship* (National Council of YMCAs, 640 Forest Road, London E17 3DZ, 1989), Section: Special Occasions, p 18.

# 47

## THEME

# Going To War
### (Remembrance Day)

**AIM**
- i) To consider some aspects of war and the suffering.
- ii) To think about various people's motives and differing attitudes towards war.

**INTRODUCTION**
Refer to the tradition of wearing a 'poppy' in remembrance of those who died in wars and battles since the First World War. Ask how many have bought a poppy.

**OPTIONS AND IDEAS**

A. Divide the class into groups. Ask them: 'Why do people go to war?' Give them two minutes to come up with as many reasons as they can. (Give them some ideas to get started, eg because someone has taken over their territory or to protect innocent people being tortured and killed). After the time spent in the groups read this short story:

229

Two soldiers lay under their blankets looking up at the stars. Says Jack, 'What made you go into the army, Tom?' 'Well,' replied Tom, 'I had no wife and I loved war, Jack, so I went. What made you go?' 'Well,' returned Jack, 'I had a wife and I loved peace, Tom, so I went.'[1]

Suggest that people may have very different motives for going to war, some may be easier to justify than others. Some Christians consider a war to be just if it is based on the following principles:

1. War can only be declared if there is a just cause.
2. The intention must be just: it must be to restore a just peace.
3. It must be the last resort, when everything else has failed.
4. There must be an official declaration of war by a legitimate power.
5. Limited objectives must be set.
6. The immunity of non-combatants must be respected.
7. Limited means must be used in proportion to the objectives you want to achieve.
8. There must be a reasonable hope of success when you start.
9. The benefit from the war must outweigh the evil of going to war.
10. There must be scope for conscientious objectors to opt out of the war.[2]

B. Read the following lines. They were probably written by a child; they were found scratched on the wall of a bomb-blasted air-raid shelter in Germany after the Second World War:

I believe in the light,
even when the sun doesn't shine.

> I believe in love,
> even when it isn't given.
>
> I believe in God,
> even when his voice is silent.[3]

Give pupils a few moments of quiet reflection on this inscription, then ask them to write down their ideas about who might have written this, what they were experiencing then and the kind of background this person might have come from. Ask them to think about the reasons why this person wrote these words.

C. Point out that most people who die in battles are between the ages of eighteen to twenty-five years old. Most of them leave grieving wives and children, fathers and mothers, brothers and sisters behind. Read the short poem 'A Scrap Of Paper' which illustrates the despair which hits people who receive the notice that their loved one has died. It is by G. A. Studdert Kennedy who was perhaps the most famous padre serving in the First World War and whose poems moved the hearts of thousands of people in that war, bringing strength and comfort to countless readers:

> Just a little scrap of paper
> In a yellow envelope,
> And the whole world is a ruin,
> Even Hope.[4]

D. Find out more about people who risk their own lives to save others. For example, Mordechai Vanunu who worked as a technician at Israel's top-secret Dimona nuclear research complex for nine years before being dismissed in 1985 for pro-Arab sympathies. He left Israel. In Australia he became friends with an Anglican clergyman and became a committed Christian. His new-found faith convinced him that he should, in the interest of world peace, expose Israel's clandestine activities. So he told the story about the inner workings of the Dimona to the editors of *The Sunday Times* which was published in October 1986. Soon retaliation hit him swiftly and ruthlessly. He was kidnapped by Mossad agents and tried behind closed doors in a Jerusalem courtroom. Convicted for espionage, treason and betraying State secrets, Vanunu was sentenced to eighteen years in prison. Despite being nominated for the Nobel Peace Prize, and having his case taken up by the European Parliament, his appeals against the sentence have been rejected. Vanunu remains in solitary confinement until the present day, forbidden to speak even to the priest who brings him communion.[5]

Ask pupils for their reaction to this story. Talk about groups of people who put their own lives at risk for the sake of others (eg firemen, police, bomb disposal experts, etc). Ask: 'Why do they do it?'

E. Some pupils may feel able to write a short prayer of thanks for those people who risk their lives for the sake of others.

## IDEAS FOR DEVELOPMENT

Look up and read some stories about innocent people who have got caught up in the horrors of a war or conflict. Read the story of the nurse Marie Wilson who was murdered by an IRA bomb during a Remembrance Day service at Enniskillen in 1987.[6]

## FOOTNOTES

[1] W. E. Thorn, *A Bit Of Honey—After-dinner Addresses Of Inspiration, Wit And Humour* (Zondervan Publishing House: Grand Rapids/Michigan, 1964), p 70.

[2] Abridged from: Margaret Cooling, *War And Pacifism—The Facts And The Choices* (Scripture Union: London, 1988), ISBN 0 86201 389 5, pp 71-72.
[3] 'I Believe' in: John Bailey (ed), *Blueprint Book Four* (Galliard/Stainer & Bell: London, 1976), ISBN 0 85249 354 1, p 1241.
[4] 'A Scrap Of Paper' in: G. A. Studdert Kennedy, *The Unutterable Beauty* (Hodder & Stoughton: London, 1927), p 79.
[5] Tom Gilling/John McKnight, *Trial & Error* (Monarch Publications: Eastbourne, 1991), ISBN 1 85424 129 X.
[6] Gordon Wilson/Alf McCreary, *Marie* (Marshall Pickering: London, 1990), ISBN 0 551 02276 0.

# 48

## THEME
# Christmas

**AIM**
To provoke thought about the Christian significance of Christmas.

**INTRODUCTION**
Brainstorm the group on what matters most to them at Christmas. Write up their ideas either on the OHP or chalkboard. Take a vote if appropriate.

**OPTION AND IDEAS**

A. Play an extract from a current Christmas 'hit' song or a prepared recording of extracts from several Christmas 'hits' would be better. Refer to songs like Cliff Richard's 'Saviour's Day' (1990) and 'Mistletoe And Wine' (1988) or Slade's ever popular 'Merry Christmas' (1973) which was reissued in 1980, 1981, 1982, 1983, 1984, 1985 and 1986! Ask what makes a No 1 Christmas song. Move on to talk about the popularity of certain Christmas carols. Find out which carols are their favourites and why.

B. Prepare two pupils to present the drama 'Father And Son':

> The scene is heaven, the moment before Christ enters the world. This sketch seeks to capture the mixed emotions that both Father and Son might have experienced.
>
> The Father is seated, busily occupied. The Son enters carrying a rucksack.
>
> SON. Father, it's nearly time to go. I think I'm ready.
>
> FATHER. (A little absent-minded) Ah, good, yes of course. You've got everything? You're all packed?
>
> SON. Yes, Father, don't worry. I've checked everything.
>
> FATHER. And double-checked?
>
> SON. And double-checked.
>
> FATHER. Only we wouldn't want you to forget anything, this *is* rather important.
>
> SON. Look for yourself. Everything I need. (Opens rucksack, turns it upside down. It is empty.)
>
> SON. See, nothing. Completely nothing.
>
> FATHER. You're sure you haven't overlooked the odd block of gold tucked away somewhere?
>
> SON. No Father.
>
> FATHER. No angel trying to hitch a free passage in the front pocket?
>
> SON. Definitely not, although I did catch a couple of 'em rehearsing for a presentation for something down there.
>
> FATHER. Yes, you will bump into the odd thousand.
>
> SON. Oh yes, and before you ask, there's nothing in my wallet either. (Opens wal-

|           | let.) See not a penny to my name. I feel rather naked really. It's strange to be so empty. |
|-----------|---|
| FATHER.   | But it's *so* important too. You must go with nothing. Completely vulnerable, that's your strength. Now, do you have the address? |
| SON.      | Yes, written down, in Hebrew. |
| FATHER.   | They're a lovely couple. Very humble people, but very poor too. |
| SON.      | But aren't they all like that down there? Do they know I'm coming? |
| FATHER.   | Yes, although I had a little difficulty with the husband; he wasn't too keen on the idea. I think the virgin birth threw him a little. |
| SON.      | I think it'll probably throw a few others too. |
| FATHER.   | Well, in the end I had to send Gabe along, that convinced him. He's got a way with dreams you know, has our Gabe. |
| SON.      | (Pulls a wad of paper from his pocket) I found this list of things. I don't understand how they fit in. (Reads) Myrrh; Gold; Incense; a towel and a bowl of water; a huge amount of bread...(amazed)...and wine! Three nails...oh and er...(Releases wad of paper, which drops into a long list, reaching the floor) rather a lot of parables. Surely I'm not to take all this along. |
| FATHER.   | No. No need. You'll find those already in place down there. They're visual aids. Which reminds me, you do know why you're going? |
| SON.      | Yes. Yes, I think so. But it's all such a huge risk. |

FATHER. That's the whole point. It wouldn't be me if it wasn't—it wouldn't be love at all. Well, it's time. Son, I want you to remember that although we're apart for a short time, we'll soon be reunited—and this sacrifice is going to count for all eternity.

SON. I know it's going to be hard to be human. I fear that there might come a point when that frailty will be too much, and I'll want to take another way out.

FATHER. I'll be with you when that happens. It's very hard to be weak when you know how strong you really are. But there'll come a time when even I must turn my back on you.

SON. You?

FATHER. But just trust me, it's the only way. And at that point of complete isolation, that will be the moment of victory. (They embrace. The Son goes to leave.)

FATHER. There *is* just one thing you must take with you. These two, empty hands. (Father takes Son's open hands.) They are all you need for a lifetime of love.
(Both freeze).[1]

Look up the Bible passage on which this work is based (Philippians 2:6–11). Ask pupils to share their ideas about the way the writer has imagined this scene. Explain that this sketch attempts to illustrate the Christian belief that God became a human person in Jesus, although it does contain some controversial ideas which need to be discussed (eg 'I think the virgin birth threw him a little' and the son's reply to 'Do you know why you are going?').

C. If possible, purchase small quantities of myrrh and frankincense which can be seen and handled by pupils.[2] Have something to represent gold. Explain to pupils the significance of these gifts brought by the magi to Jesus:[3]

> *Frankincense:* The resin gives off a sweet scent when warmed or burned and was used as incense (ie a costly offering and a sign of acknowledgment of deity). This gift presented to Jesus by the magi symbolises his role as a priest who helps people to become friends with God.
> *Gold:* A very precious metal. It is an appropriate gift for a king.
> *Myrrh:* Used as a spice and as a medicine: a painkiller. On the cross Jesus was offered wine mixed with myrrh, and later his body was embalmed. It indicated suffering, pain and death.

What gift would they consider appropriate to offer this special baby?

## IDEAS FOR DEVELOPMENT
Find out when and how Russian Orthodox Christians in the East celebrate Jesus' birth.[4]

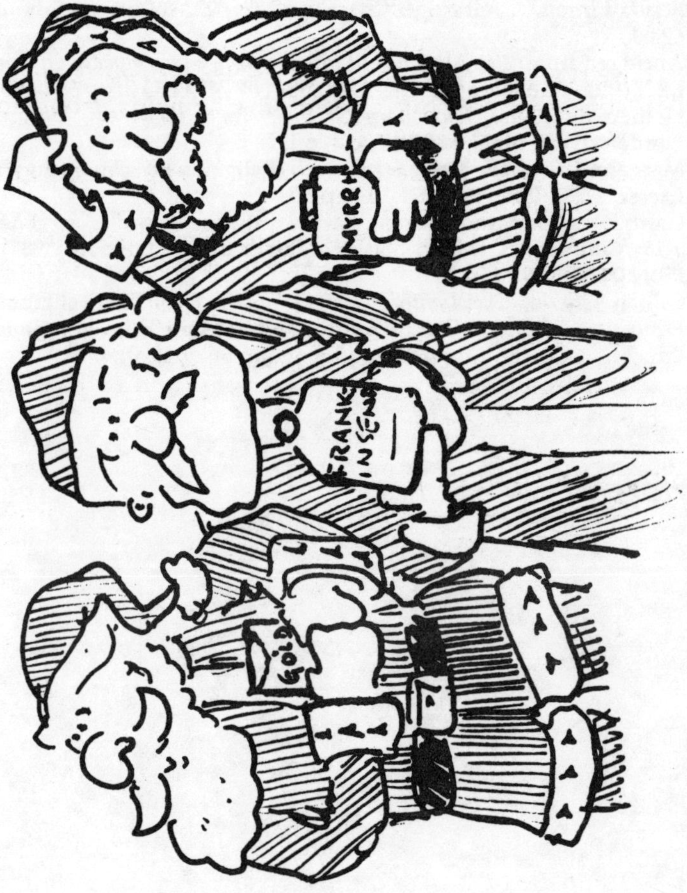
MYRRH
FRANK
GOLD

## FOOTNOTES

[1] 'Father And Son' in: Dave Hopwood, *Acting On Impulse* (Lee Abbey: Lynton, 1987), pp 22-23.

[2] Small quantities of frankincense and myrrh obtainable from Culpeper Stores or by mail order from Culpeper Ltd, Hadstock Road, Linton, Cambridge CB1 6NJ, Tel: 0223-891196 for about £2.00.

[3] Abridged from: Pat Alexander (ed), *The Lion Encyclopedia Of The Bible* (Lion Publishing: Tring, 1978), ISBN 0 7459 1113 7, pp 689-690.
Herbert Sundemo, *Dictionary Of Bible Times* (Scripture Union: London, 1979), ISBN 0 85421 538 7, p 132.

[4] Margaret Doak, *The Orthodox Church* (Religious Education Press: Exeter, 1978), ISBN 0 08 021410 X, p 50.
Garth Read/John Rudge/Roger B. Howarth, *The Westhill Project RE 5-16: Christians 3* (Mary Glasgow Publications: London, 1987), ISBN 0 86158 696 4, p 8.
Gillian Crowe, *Christianity—The Orthodox Tradition* (Religious Education Teachers' Centre/South London Multi-Faith Religious Education Centre, Kilmorie Road, London SE23, 1990), p 38.

# 49

## THEME

# EASTER 1—Good Friday

**AIM**

To explore the Christian significance of Jesus' death.

**INTRODUCTION**

Bring in one rusty nail for every pupil. Refer to crucifixion as a particularly horrific method of execution. Ask the pupils to have a good look at their nail. Let them feel it in reflective silence. If appropriate, play a piece of sombre music.[1]

**OPTIONS AND IDEAS**

A. Ask the pupils to share their feelings in small groups of two or three: Ask pupils to think about why Christians believe that Jesus was willing to endure such a painful death. After they have had a few moments to consider this question look up the following two passages to illustrate the Biblical explanation: Isaiah 53:5–6 and Romans 5:6–8.

B. Read the story 'Someone Else's Spanking':

> When I was four years old, my parents had a lovely antique table, on which the telephone rested. One day I threw a temper tantrum so violent that I tried to think of a desperate act to express my irritation. I took a wicked and forbidden object, a kitchen knife, and with fierce determination, hit this small table repeatedly, leaving deep gashes in the antique wood. The inevitable result descended at suppertime. I guess my poor mama had been too rushed to see the table, but dad soon noticed.
> 'Who did this?' he boomed. No use cowering. My guilt was established. Suddenly there was an unexpected turn of events. Eight-year-old Priscilla felt compassion for her now submissive small sister. 'Dad,' Priscilla said, 'I want to take Susan's spanking this time.'
> The whole family was thunderstruck by the offer. I was provided with a lifelong lesson when, after some anxious consultation, my parents reluctantly concluded that it was a fair offer.
> I'll never forget the spanking my sister took for me. The knife gashes had been paid for by somebody else's love for me.[2]

Compare this story with the Christian belief that when Jesus died on the cross he died in their place and suffered the death-penalty due for their wrong-doing.

C. Refer to recent hostages such as Terry Waite, John McCarthy and Brian Keenan. Explain that these men were civilians who were captured in Lebanon and then held as prisoners. Hostages are often used as 'bargaining counters' (ie they are seen by the captors as security and may be 'returned' only in exchange for something they want). Conduct a mock 'hostage exchange'. Be sensitive in your choice of subject for this—a teacher may be persuaded to take this role! Prepare some 'bargaining terms'. Write on the board what people are willing to offer in exchange. Ensure that you drive a hard bargain for the release of the 'hostage'.

D. Christians believe that people are in debt to God because they have not lived up to God's standards but that Jesus's death was the price paid for their release. Write an imaginary bill (ie an IOU)—with 'paid by Jesus Christ, date: Good Friday, place: Golgotha—Jerusalem' stamp on it.

E. Use the following presentation ideas to write a rap with the whole group on the story of Jesus' crucifixion (Matthew 27:45–51,54). Perform it in a main assembly:

—With two pieces of cloth, sheets or blankets (which you don't mind ripping) make a closed-in place, representing the spot in the temple where God was present.
—Darken the room if possible.
—Have a camera with a flash ready.

(Hammering)

That afternoon, the whole earth was covered with darkness (switch off light/darken the room) for three hours, from noon until three o'clock. About three o'clock Jesus (character 1) shouted, 'Eli, Eli, lama sabachthani,' which means, 'My God, my God, why have you forsaken me?'
Some of the bystanders misunderstood and thought he was calling for Elijah. One of them ran (noise of running in sand) and filled a sponge (water running noise) with sour wine and put it on a stick and held it up to him to drink. But the rest (several characters) said, 'Leave him alone. Let's see whether Elijah will come and save him.'

Then Jesus shouted out again, (character 1 shouts) dismissed his spirit and died. And look! The curtain secluding the Holiest Place in the Temple was split apart from top to bottom (ripping of the two sheets); and the earth shook (drums/camera flashes), and rocks broke (tumbling noises). The soldiers at the crucifixion and their sergeant were terribly frightened by the earthquake and all that happened. They exclaimed, 'Surely this was God's Son.'

F. Some pupils may like an opportunity to use the following prayer called 'Thoughts On Good Friday' written by a pupil from a comprehensive school in Bristol:

Dear Jesus,
I suppose everybody should have expected
you'd have to die.
That's what usually happens to people
who talk sense and nobody wants to listen.
They don't like people to be different.
But there was more to it than that.
It was some sort of plan.
I find it all very puzzling.
If you were a ransom, Lord,
who were you paying it to?
It wasn't being paid to the devil, was it?
Was it to God?
I didn't think God was like that.
But I suppose he has to keep the rules, too,
even if he made them.
It showed how much you loved us though
and that's what really matters.
And I like the bit where you forgave everybody.
But, anyway, Jesus,
there's one thing I know:
you died for me.
Thanks.[3]

## IDEAS FOR DEVELOPMENT
Find hymns which major on the different aspects of the meaning of Jesus Christ's death.

## FOOTNOTES
[1] Gustav Mahler, *Symphony No 5 In C Sharp Minor Adagietto*. Rachmaninov, *Piano Concerto No 2*. Slow movement.
[2] 'Someone Else's Spanking' in: Susan Schaeffer Macaulay, *How To Be Your Own Selfish Pig* (Scripture Union: London, 1982), ISBN 0 86201 161 2, pp 74-75. Used with permission by David C. Cook Publishing Company.
[3] Abridged from 'Thoughts On Good Friday' in: Janet Green, *Home-made Prayers* (Lion Publishing: Tring, 1983), ISBN 0 85848 211 0, p 72.

# 50
### THEME

# EASTER 2—
# The Resurrection

**AIM**

To think about the significance of the resurrection in terms of new life and the joy that it brings.

**INTRODUCTION**

Bring in something to symbolise new life (eg an egg, a kitten or if you live in the country perhaps a local farmer or parent could bring in a new lamb; alternatively a young mother might be willing to bring in her baby). If no living example is possible then collect some pictures or slides of new life. Talk about the joy, excitement and hope that new life can bring. Allow pupils an opportunity to talk about their experience of new life (eg a baby brother or sister, a pet, etc).

**OPTIONS AND IDEAS**

A. Link the ideas about new life with the tradition of giving and receiving chocolate eggs or decorated eggs at Easter time. Invite pupils to share their knowledge and ideas about the Christian festival of Easter. Check your facts against the story of Jesus' crucifixion (Good Friday) and his resurrection (Easter Sunday) as found in one of the Gospels (Luke 23:13—24:12). Emphasise the point that the Easter Egg is a symbol of the resurrection, ie the shell is like the tomb where Jesus' body was put after his crucifixion, and the chick hatching out is, for Christians, a reminder of Jesus bursting out of the tomb in new life. If possible, obtain a copy of the video 'Jesus' and show the relevant clip of the scene at the Garden tomb on the first Easter Sunday.[1]

B. Explain that the Gospel accounts present the story of the resurrection as a fact. Central to the story is the empty tomb and the disappearance of the body of Jesus. What could have happened to it? Put pupils into groups and give them two minutes to consider together what might have happened to the body. Get them to report back. (They may need prompting with some ideas, eg the disciples stole the body, the authorities removed it, the women went to the wrong tomb, he wasn't really dead, etc.) Look at the weaknesses in these ideas.[2]

C. Christians all over the world celebrate Easter Sunday in a variety of ways. Read pupils the following account of one such celebration written by Michael Bordeaux who studied in Moscow. He recalls the excitement of the Easter midnight service at a church in Moscow:

> I was standing in the church in total darkness. Although I was protected in a little enclosure at the front I knew the church must be full.... I could feel the tension, the spiritual expectancy, which the faithful generated.... Then the sound of a distant mournful chant. It grew louder as the deacons and priests approached the main door: 'They have taken away my Lord and I know not where they have laid

him.' A hammering and creaking from the back indicated a great door opening. 'Whom seek ye?' 'The body of Jesus.' 'Why seek ye the living among the dead? He is not here. He is risen—Khristos voskrese!' For the first time the great crowd broke its silence. A murmur, as though they could not believe the truth they were affirming: Voistinu voskrese ('Is risen indeed') was their antiphon. But now too there was light. Someone at the back had lit the first paschal candle, a single point of light not able to penetrate the darkness. But then there was another, and another. Swiftly the flame passed from hand to hand. I began to see what I had not known. Every one of the worshippers held a candle. In less than a minute the church was a blaze of light—no, not the impersonal glare of electricity—it was five thousand individual flames united in one faith. Each candle lit up a face behind it. That face bore the deep lines of sorrow, or personal tragedy. Yet, as it was illuminated, the suffering turned to joy, to the certain knowledge of the reality of the risen Lord.[3]

D. Christians believe that because Jesus rose from the dead they too will live again after physical death. Jesus said: 'For I will live again—and you will too' (John 14:19b). Pope John Paul II has coined the phrase 'The Easter People' for Christians, because of their belief in this new life. Divide the class into two groups and ask each group to write a script for a radio programme called 'Easter People' with interviews, either from Mary Magdalene or some disciples who claim to have seen Jesus (Luke 24 or John 20,21). Alternatively, pupils could write up an imaginary interview with the wife of the former Archbishop Janani Luwum. He was killed in a car accident. (It is suspected that this was the plot of President Idi Amin.)[4]

E. Pupils might enjoy singing a rousing Easter hymn like 'Yours Be The Glory', a traditional French song like 'Now The Green Blade Riseth' or 'Led Like A Lamb' by Graham Kendrick.[5]

**IDEAS FOR DEVELOPMENT**
Organise a competition for the best decorated egg.

**FOOTNOTES**

[1] *Jesus—The Life That Changed History* (Campus Crusade for Christ/International Films, The Coach House, 55 Drayton Green, London W13 0JD). Video. Duration: 110 minutes.

[2] John Austin Baker, *Evidence For The Resurrection* (Mowbray: Oxford, 1986), ISBN 0 264 67113 9.
Michael Green, *The Day Death Died* (Inter-Varsity Press: Leicester, 1982), ISBN 0 85110 438 X.
Brenda Courtie/Margaret Johnson, *Christianity Explored* (Lion Publishing: Oxford, 1990), ISBN 0 7459 1800 X, pp 56-59.
Val Grieve, *Your Verdict* (STL Books: Bromley, 1988), ISBN 1 85078 036 6.

[3] Abridged from: Mary Batchelor (compiler), *The Lion Easter Book* (Lion Publishing: Tring, 1987), ISBN 0 85648 945 X, p 45.

[4] *ibid* pp 58-59.
David Self, *Stories From The Christian World* (Macdonald: London, 1986), ISBN 0 356 11508 9, pp 40-41.
John Godwin, *Still More Lives To Inspire* (Moorley's Publishing: Ilkeston, 1987), ISBN 0 86071 260 5, pp 58-59.

[5] 'Yours Be The Glory!' in: Peter Horrobin/Greg Leavers (compilers), *Junior Praise* (Marshall Pickering: Basingstoke, 1986), ISBN 0 551 01293 5, No 299.
'Now The Green Blade Riseth' in: Fred Pratt Green/Allen Percival et al, *Partners In Praise* (Galliard/Stainer & Bell: London, 1979), ISBN 0 85249 555 2, No 81. Or in: *The Oxford Book Of Carols* (Oxford University Press: Oxford, 1964), No 149.
'Led Like A Lamb' in: *Songs & Hymns Of Fellowship* (Kingsway: Eastbourne, 1987), ISBN 0 86065 528 8, No 307.

# 51

## THEME

# Ascension

**AIM**
i) To consider the Christian belief that the life of Jesus would be incomplete without the ascension.
ii) To show the importance of the supernatural dimension of the Christian faith.

**INTRODUCTION**
Tell the group that you want them to imagine that one of their friends claims to have been present when one of the group disappeared 'before their very eyes'. They haven't seen him since, but claim he is still alive. Ask: 'How would you react to this story?' 'Would you believe your friend?' 'Why/Why not?'

**OPTIONS AND IDEAS**

A. Tell them that this story was similar to the story about Jesus and his ascension. Look up the story in Acts 1:9–13. The disciples were with Jesus, listening to him talking, when he disappeared from their sight. Many Christians believe that this really happened and that Jesus is still alive today, even though he is not visible, and one day he will reign over all the earth. Then and only then, the story will be complete.

B. Split the class into groups and play the Cutting Out Game:

> You will need old magazines or old newspapers and some pairs of scissors, glue and a large sheet of paper. Look for stories that talk about certain things or kinds of people. Decide that you don't believe in these things or in the existence of these people and cut out wherever they are mentioned.
>
> Example:
> You are going to decide that you don't believe that foreign countries or foreign people exist. You believe that only your own country exists. So you have to cut out everything that mentions another country or products or people from another country. Then paste together what remains from your newspaper or magazine on a large sheet of paper. Now try and read the article, full of gaps, to another group. Can they make sense of it?[1]

Talk about this exercise. Point out that a lot of people cut out from the Bible the supernatural aspects of the resurrection or the ascension of Jesus and act as if the rest of it and of Jesus' life makes sense by itself. A modern Christian poet expresses this in the following poem 'The Critic':

He wanted a Jesus
For the twentieth-century flocks,
A saviour fit
To be a superstar.
He left miracles and faith

> On the cutting-room floor:
> But his Gospel
> Was abridged too far...[2]

C. Discuss the statement 'seeing is believing'. Make a list of other invisible things which we believe are there, eg electricity, radio or TV waves, high notes which we cannot hear.

D. Do the following experiment to show that some things do exist that cannot be seen: light a candle in front of the class and put a glass jar on top. The candle will blow out. Ask: 'What happened?' 'Why?' (The jar on top cuts out oxygen). 'Where is the oxygen?' Oxygen is invisible but with a scientific experiment we can show that it is there.

E. Show that even one of the disciples, Thomas, said that he wouldn't believe that Jesus had risen from the dead unless he could see Jesus and touch him himself: 'When they [the disciples] kept telling him [Thomas], "We have seen the Lord," he replied, "I won't believe it unless I see the nail wounds in his hands—and put my fingers into them—and place my hand into his side" ' (John 20:25). Explain that eight days after this, Thomas had his chance to see and actually touch Jesus in person. Faced with this indisputable evidence, Thomas was quick to accept that it really was Jesus. The Bible records Jesus' words to Thomas (John 20:29): 'You believe because you have seen me. But blessed are those who haven't seen me and believe anyway.'

Ask pupils to think what their reaction would have been if they had been in Thomas' shoes. Would they have believed the reports from other disciples that Jesus was alive without seeing him for themselves? 'Why/why not?'

## IDEAS FOR DEVELOPMENT
Make a newspaper article about the ascension.
Investigate the invisibility of electricity with its visible effects.

## FOOTNOTES
[1] 'Cutting Out' adapted from: Francis & Edith Schaeffer, *Everybody Can Know* (Tyndale House Publishers: Wheaton/Illinois, 1973), ISBN 8423 0785 0, p 72.
[2] 'The Critic' in: Gerard Kelly, *Rebel Without Applause—Barbed Verse For A Comfortable World* (Minstrel/Monarch: Eastbourne, 1991), ISBN 1 85424 132 X, p 34.

# 52

### THEME
# Pentecost

**AIM**

To consider the Christian significance of two symbols of Pentecost—wind and fire—and their potential for change.

**INTRODUCTION**

Have some pictures or reports to show the effects of high winds and disastrous fire. Show how they are powerful forces for change (eg forest fires, shipwrecks).

**OPTIONS AND IDEAS**

A. Explain that wind and fire are both symbols of the Holy Spirit and are mentioned in the Bible story about the Day of Pentecost, when the Holy Spirit was given to the church. Talk about the background to Pentecost: The awful events surrounding Jesus' arrest and crucifixion were still fresh in the minds of the disciples. They had been in despair. Then on Easter Sunday morning they were excited as news of Jesus' resurrection began to spread, and as they saw him and talked with him, hope was renewed. Then, suddenly, he was gone again. They saw him disappear in the heavens, and they heard Jesus' instructions that they were to return to Jerusalem and wait there for the promised gift—the coming of the Holy Spirit. About one hundred and twenty of Jesus' followers, friends and members of his family were waiting together in a large upstairs room in Jerusalem. They probably spent much of their time going over the events of the past few weeks and prayed together and read from the Old Testament Scriptures. And then the following happened:

> Suddenly there was a sound like the roaring of a mighty windstorm in the skies above them and it filled the house where they were meeting. Then, what looked like flames or tongues of fire appeared and settled on their heads. And everyone present was filled with the Holy Spirit and began speaking in languages they didn't know, for the Holy Spirit gave them this ability. Many godly Jews were in Jerusalem that day for the religious celebrations, having arrived from many nations. And when they heard the roaring in the sky above the house, crowds came running to see what it was all about, and were stunned to hear their own languages being spoken by the disciples. 'How can this be?' they exclaimed. 'For these men are all from Galilee, and yet we hear them speaking all the native languages of the lands where we were born! And we all hear these men telling in our own languages about the mighty miracles of God!' They stood there amazed and perplexed. 'What can this mean?' they asked each other. But others in the crowd were mocking. 'They're drunk, that's all!' they said. Then Peter stepped forward with the eleven apostles and

shouted to the crowd, 'Listen, all of you, visitors and residents alike! Some of you are saying these men are drunk! It isn't true! It's much too early for that! People don't get drunk by 9 am!' (Acts 2:2–8,11–15).

Then Peter went on to preach his first great sermon! At the end of it, around 3,000 people decided to accept Peter's words and they outwardly expressed their desire to become followers of Jesus too.

Write up the word 'wind' and then ask pupils to tell you what it feels like to be out in it (eg to be blown around or swept along by its power and strength). Then ask them to try to imagine why the Holy Spirit is likened to the wind (ie the Spirit's power to change people and enable them, etc). Talk about the properties of 'fire' in the same way (ie refining cleansing properties of fire should be emphasised and linked with the purifying effects of the Spirit on believers). Pupils may enjoy designing a banner or a flag which incorporates the wind and fire symbols of the Holy Spirit.

B. Tell pupils that they are to imagine themselves as a TV news reporter in Jerusalem. They have been assigned the task of producing a report on events in down-town Jerusalem for the *Six O'Clock News*. Suggest that they should try to get an interview with one of the disciples and some eyewitness accounts from the crowd. Let them work on this in small groups.

C. Show the class some 'Before and After' pictures (eg someone who has lost weight, someone who used a particular shampoo, etc). Alternatively, bring out the idea of the change in Peter through role play, ie you or a competent pupil go outside the room, then peep in pretending to be afraid of so many people. Talk about Peter being afraid to face people with the truth about his friendship with Jesus. Then, through role play, show 'Peter' as a completely different character—jumping around, enthusiastically waving his hands, telling everyone very boldly about the good news that Jesus has risen from the dead. Ask pupils what brought about the change in Peter. Working in pairs, ask pupils to produce a 'Before' and 'After' profile of Peter to show the dramatic changes that occurred after he received the Holy Spirit at Pentecost. Give them the following information to help them.

*Before* Pentecost Peter denied knowing Jesus (Mark 14:66–72) and with other disciples hid behind locked doors (John 20:19).

*After* Pentecost he went out on the streets preaching (Acts 2:14), and risking imprisonment (Acts 12:1–5), stood up to the Council and High Priest (Acts 5:27–32).

D. If appropriate, sing the song 'For I'm Building A People Of Power' together.[1] Alternatively, listen to the beautiful call for the Holy Spirit in the Yoruba language from Nigeria called 'Wa Wa Emimimo' which can be sung excitedly or meditatively.[2]

## IDEAS FOR DEVELOPMENT

Find out about the Jewish Festival of Pentecost or the way the Church celebrates Pentecost or Whitsun today.[3]

Make cards, posters, banners to celebrate Pentecost as the birthday of the church.

## FOOTNOTES

[1] 'For I'm Building A People Of Power' in: Peter Horrobin/Greg Leavers (compilers), *Junior Praise* (Marshall Pickering: Basingstoke, 1986), ISBN 0 551 01293 5, No 47.

[2] 'Wa Wa Wa Emimimo' in: John L. Bell (ed), *Many & Great—Songs Of The World Church 1* (Wild Goose Publications: Glasgow, 1990), ISBN 0 947988 40 8, p 42. Available on tape: *Many & Great* (Wild Goose Publications: Glasgow).

[3] Sue Penney, *Discovering Religions: Judaism* (Heinemann Educational: Oxford, 1987), ISBN 0 435 30301 5, pp 28-29.

Maureen Austerberry, *The Westhill Project RE 5-16: Jews 2* (Stanley Thornes: Cheltenham, 1990), ISBN 1 871402 19 0, p 26.

Angela Wood, *Looking Into World Religions: Being A Jew* (Batsford: London, 1987), ISBN 0 7134 4668 4, pp 38-40.

Clive Lawton, *Religions Through Festivals: Judaism* (Longman: Harlow, 1989), ISBN 0 582 31790 8, pp 38-39.

Fay Sampson, *Living Festivals: Ascensiontide And Pentecost* (Religious and Moral Education Press: Exeter, 1986), ISBN 0 08 031774 X.

R. O. Hughes, *Religions Through Festivals: Christianity* (Longman: Harlow, 1989), ISBN 0 582 31791 6, pp 34-35.

# FURTHER SUGGESTIONS

## A HELPING HAND

Hugh Patterson, *Time Together* (Macdonald/Religious and Moral Education Press: Exeter, 1983), ISBN 0 356 09218 6/0 08 036036 X, pp 81-83. Assembly outline: 'Helping Others'.

Charles Moreton, *Time To Grow—Book 2* (Angel Press: Chichester, 1985), ISBN 0 947785 05 1, pp 5-7. Assembly outline: 'Working Together'.

Elizabeth Peirce, *Activity Assemblies For Christian Collective Worship 5 To 11* (The Falmer Press: Basingstoke, 1991), ISBN 1 85000 729 2, pp 81-102. Assembly outlines and ideas on 'People Who Need Help'.

Glyn Jones, *Good Morning, Children!* (Edward Arnold: Leeds, 1980), ISBN 0 560 00802 3, pp 243-254. Readings on 'Helping Others'.

*Images* (The Woodcraft Folk, 13 Ritherdon Road, London SW17 8QE). Resource Pack.

Alan Millard, *Ideas For Assemblies* (Cambridge University Press: Cambridge, 1990), ISBN 0 521 38889 9, pp 1-7. Seven assembly outlines on 'Working Together'.

## MAKING CHANGES

'Change Of Heart' in: Potters Clay Drama, *Act One* (M Video Services/Potters Clay Communications, 17 Shelley Drive,

Lutterworth, Leics LE17 4XF, 1984), pp 32-34. Sketch.

*From Crime To Christ* (CTA/GAV Services, 21 Cheviot Close, Ramsbottom, Bury, Lancs BL0 9LL). This thirty-minute documentary-style video tells the stories of four men who after lives of crime and time in prison have been transformed by the life-changing power of Jesus. Some share about their involvement in helping ex-offenders. Shot at Strangeways Prison in Manchester.

Jan Thompson, *Reflecting* (Hodder & Stoughton: Sevenoaks, 1988), ISBN 0 340 42954 2, pp 4-7. Two assembly outlines.

Tony Jasper (ed), *Moments Of Truth* (Marshall Pickering: London, 1990), ISBN 0 551 01876 3. A collection of spiritual turning points in the lives of well-known Christians.

## GOOD NEIGHBOURS

Dave Hopwood, *Child's Play* (In Sight, 56 Booker Lane, High Wycombe, Bucks HP12 3UY, 1990), p 33. Sketch 'Good Sam'.

Linda Hoy/Mike Hoy, *An Alternative Assembly Book* (Longman: Harlow, 1985), ISBN 0 582 36124 9, pp 11-20. Five assembly outlines on 'Who Is My Neighbour?'

June Tillman, *The Oxford Assembly Book* (Oxford University Press: Oxford, 1989), ISBN 0 19 321775 9, pp 110-122. Songs, poems, readings and discussion topics on 'Our Neighbourhood' including the wider community.

Alan Millard, *Ideas For Assemblies* (Cambridge University Press: Cambridge, 1990), ISBN 0 521 38889 9, pp 47-52. Six assembly outlines on 'Community'.

## BEING WRONG

Colin Chapman, *The Case For Christianity* (Lion Publishing: Tring, 1981), ISBN 0 85648 371 0, pp 20-21,49-52, 94-101,113,122. General reading with lots of quotations.

*Turning Point* (Scripture Union, 130 City Road, London EC1V 2NJ). A twelve-minute photographic documentary about Muslim and Hindu converts to Christianity, in video or soundstrip format.

Derek Haylock, *Acts For Apostles* (Church House Publishing:

London, 1987), ISBN 0 7151 0446 2, pp 49-53. Sketch based on Jesus' statement: 'The Way'.

## JACKSTRAWS

Gordon & Ronni Lamont, *Move Yourselves* (Bible Society: Swindon, 1983), ISBN 0 564 07292 3, pp 53-58. Exploring the Bible passage (1 Corinthians 12) through mime: 'Contact Work'.

Pip Wilson, *Games Without Frontiers* (Marshall Pickering: Basingstoke, 1988), ISBN 0 551 01554 3, pp 31-58. Group participation games.

Tony Rousell, *Our Turn For Assembly* (Basil Blackwell: Oxford, 1985), ISBN 0 631 13664 9, pp 57-62. Assembly outline on 'We All Have A Part To Play'.

*Winners All* (Pax Christi, 9 Henry Road, London N4 2LH, 1980), ISBN 0 9506757 1 7. Cooperative games for all ages.

## ACHIEVEMENT

John Godwin, *Still More Lives To Inspire—Stories For School Assemblies* (Moorley's Publishing: Ilkeston, 1987), ISBN 0 86071 260 5. Assembly outlines on famous Christian people.

Redvers Brandling, *It Makes You Think—Discussion Themes For Class And Assembly* (Edward Arnold: London, 1985), ISBN 0 7131 7317 3, pp 58-64. Assembly outline on determination.

Rowland Purton, *Assemblies* (Basil Blackwell: Oxford, 1979), ISBN 0 631 19740 0, p 157. Assembly outline on extraordinary achievements.

Barbara Wintersgill/Janet Dyson, *Life, The Universe And You* (Longman: Harlow, 1990), ISBN 0 582 02669 5, pp 28-37. RE/PSE book with chapters on achievement and potential.

## THE BIBLE

David Downton/Mike Sandy, *Showing The Way* (Moorley's Publishing: Ilkeston, 1989), ISBN 0 86071 297 4, pp 6-7. Assembly outline.

Peter Curtis, *The Christians' Book—Chichester Project 6* (Lutterworth Educational: Guildford, 1984), ISBN 0 7188 2576 4. RE textbook.

Linda Smith, *All About Living 1* (Lion Publishing: Tring, 1986), ISBN 0 7459 1160 9, pp 29-34. RE textbook.

Janet Green, *Considering Origins—Book One* (Bible Society: Swindon, 1989), ISBN 0 564 05305 8. RE textbook.

Janet Green, *Considering Meaning—Book Two* (Bible Society: Swindon, 1989), ISBN 0 564 05315 5. RE textbook.

Hugh Patterson, *Time Together* (Macdonald/Religious and Moral Education Press: London, 1983), ISBN 0 356 09218 6/0 08 036036 X, pp 156-158. Assembly outline.

'Best Seller' in: Jim Belben/Trevor Cooper, *Everyone's A Winner* (Bible Society: Swindon, 1987), ISBN 0 564 07782 8, pp 49-53. Game.

*Messages From The Memorybanks—Schools' Edition* (Bible Society: Swindon, 1988). This video consists of three twenty-minute programmes on the origins, transmission and nature of the Bible.

# CONSEQUENCES

Tony Rousell, *Our Turn For Assembly* (Basil Blackwell: Oxford, 1985), ISBN 0 631 13664 9, pp 82-87. Assembly outline on 'Consideration'.

Margaret Cooling, *Christianity Topic Book One* (Religious and Moral Education Press: Norwich, 1991), ISBN 0 900274 23 9, p 49. 'Chain Poems' and other activities.

Jill MacKredie, *Time To Reflect...* (Partnership Press: Fareham, 1990), ISBN 0 9516436 06, pp 44-46. Three secondary assembly outlines.

# WORRY

'Trust in God' in: Anthony P. Castle, *Quotes & Anecdotes—An Anthology For Preachers & Teachers* (Kevin Mayhew: Bury, 1979), ISBN 0 905725 69 7, pp 197-199.

'You Care For These Starlings' in: Ulrich Schaffer, *Into Your Light* (Inter-Varsity Press: Leicester, 1979), ISBN 0 85110 626 9. Poem.

John Bailey (ed), *Blueprint Book Four* (Stainer & Bell/Galliard: London, 1976), ISBN 0 85249 632 X, pp 1307-1319. Readings.

Meryl Doney, *The Very Worried Sparrow* (Lion Publishing: Tring, 1978), ISBN 0 85648 172 6. Picture book with a story that might appeal to secondary pupils.

## BE YOURSELF

'Healing Poem' in: Gerard Kelly, *Rebel Without Applause* (Minstrel/Monarch: Eastbourne, 1991), ISBN 1 85424 132 X, p 56.

'The Eagle And The Jackdaw' in: Russell Profitt/Valerie Bishop, *Hand In Hand Assembly Book* (Longman: Harlow, 1983), ISBN 0 582 18460 6, p 47. One of Aesop's fables.

Angela Wood, *Assembly Kit* (BBC/Longman: Harlow, 1991), ISBN 0 582 06783 9, pp 155-163. Assembly material on 'The Real Me'.

Veronica Williams, *Human Beliefs—Personal Values* (Christian Education Movement: Derby, 1991), ISBN 1 85100 031 3, pp 9-11. PSE/RE textbook.

## THE DISASTER MOVIE

M. A. Chignell, *Framework—Christianity And Life* (Edward Arnold: London, 1987), ISBN 0 7131 7526 5, pp 61-65. RE textbook with a chapter on 'Authority And Opposition'.

Ralph Gower, *Frontiers* (Lion Publishing: revised edition, Tring, 1983), ISBN 0 7459 1235 4, pp 47-49. RE textbook with a chapter on 'Authority'.

Linda Smith, *All About Living 3* (Lion Publishing: Tring, 1986), ISBN 0 7459 1162 5, pp 2-40. RE textbook on 'Law'.

Peter Curtis/Carol Smith, *Folens RE—Thinking About Living* (Folens: Dunstable, 1990), ISBN 1 85276 093 1, pp 26-27. RE textbook with a chapter on 'Authority'.

## SELFISHNESS

John Bailey (ed), *Blueprint Book Four* (Galliard/Stainer & Bell: London, 1976), ISBN 0 85249 354 1, pp 1061-1069.

David Downton/Mike Sandy, *Showing The Way* (Moorley's

Publishing: Ilkeston, 1989), ISBN 0 86071 297 4, pp 74-75. Assembly outline.

R. H. Lloyd, *More Assembly Services* (Religious Education Press: Exeter, 1975), ISBN 0 08 019889 9, pp 5-7.

'A Question Of Values' in: Gerard Kelly, *Rebel Without Applause* (Minstrel/Monarch: Eastbourne, 1991), ISBN 1 85424 132 X.

# THE POWER OF ATTRACTION

*Words Into Action* (BBC Television in association with CTVC, Beeson's Yard, Bury Lane, Rickmansworth, Herts WD3 1DS). A video of five fast moving and contemporary programmes for teenagers about the Christian faith, presented by Radio One disc jockey Simon Mayo. The last episode is about how people view Jesus, with a sketch by the *Riding Lights Theatre Company*, interviews with people of other faiths about their view of Jesus, and soccer star Glen Hoddle explains how he became interested in Christianity.

*Mark Time* (Scripture Union, 130 City Road, London EC1V 2NJ, 1989). Five stories on video, written by David Lewis and told by Roy Castle, which take us through the life of Jesus as seen through the eyes of the Roman army, emphasising the authority and power of Jesus.

Bernard Jackson, *Places Of Pilgrimage* (Geoffrey Chapman/Cassell: London, 1989), ISBN 0 225 66534 4. General information on fourteen European places.

'The Incomparable Christ' in: Bob Moffett, *Crowdmakers* (Marshall-Pickering: London, 1985), ISBN 0 7208 0588 0, pp 119-120. Poem.

# DREAMS AND SCHEMES

Linda Smith/Isobel Vale, *Work And The World* (Lion Publishing: Tring, 1988), ISBN 0 7459 1267 2, pp 12-14. PSE/RE textbook on 'What Do I Want To Do With My Life?'

Linda Hoy/Mike Hoy, *An Alternative Assembly Book* (Longman: Harlow, 1985), ISBN 0 582 36124 9, pp 128-137. Five assembly outlines on 'Dreams'.

Peter D. Smith (ed), *Peace Offerings* (Stainer & Bell: London,

1986), ISBN 0 85249 632 X, p 16. Famous speech by Martin Luther King: 'I Have A Dream'.

Sylvia Brimer, *Themes For Assembly* (Blackie & Sons: Glasgow, 1982), ISBN 0 216 91339 X, p 136. Assembly outline on 'Caedmon'.

Dorothy Taylor, *Exploring Red Letter Days* (Lutterworth Educational: Guildford, 1981), ISBN 0 7188 2479 2, pp 104-106. Assembly outline on 'A Dream Comes True'.

Glyn Jones, *Good Morning, Children!* (Edward Arnold: Leeds, 1980), ISBN 0 560 00802 3, pp 239-240. Reading 'How A Dream Came True' on Dick Whittington.

## JIGSAW

John D. Searle, *On The Right Track—Contemporary Christians In Sport* (Marshall Pickering: Basingstoke, 1987), ISBN 0 551 01424 5. Stories of famous sportsmen and women who have committed their lives to Jesus.

Ruth Harrison, *Heroes* (Lion Publishing: Oxford, 1990), ISBN 0 7459 1579 5, pp 30-31. PSE/RE textbook, exploring the meaning of life and some people's feelings that there is a hole inside them.

'The Missing Piece' in: Gordon Bailey, *Stuff And Nonsense* (Lion Publishing: Oxford, 1989), ISBN 0 7459 1828 X, p 54. Poem.

Tony Jasper (ed), *Moments Of Truth* (Marshall Pickering: London, 1990), ISBN 0 551 01876 3. A collection of stories about well-known Christians who found fulfilment in the Christian faith.

## WATER

Tony Rousell, *Our Turn For Assembly* (Basil Blackwell: Oxford, 1985), ISBN 0 631 13664 9, p 12. Assembly outline.

Simon Jenkins, *A World Of Difference* (Lion Publishing: Tring, 1988), ISBN 0 7459 1337 7, pp 15-20. PSE/RE textbook.

Elizabeth Peirce, *Activity Assemblies For Christian Collective Worship 5 to 11* (The Falmer Press: Basingstoke, 1991), ISBN 1 85000 729 2, pp 146-171. Nine assemblies on 'Water'.

## THE SENSES

*Educating For Spiritual Growth* (Church School Governors Training Programme/College of St Mark and St John, Derriford Road, Plymouth PL6 8BH). This video contains a short sequence showing a biology field trip where the children are encouraged to explore the natural environment (eg a tree) using their senses in a creative fashion.

Gillian Crowe, *Christianity—The Orthodox Tradition* (Religious Education Teachers' Centre/South London Multi-Faith Religious Education Centre, Kilmorie Road, London SE23, 1990), pp 9-11. Resource Pack with ideas how the Orthodox Church worship using all the senses.

Jill MacKredie, *Time To Reflect...* (Partnership Press: Fareham, 1990), ISBN 0 9516436 0 6, p 28. Assembly outline.

Elizabeth Peirce, *Activity Assemblies For Christian Collective Worship 5 to 11* (The Falmer Press: Basingstoke, 1991), ISBN 1 85000 729 2, pp 187-207. Five assemblies, exploring our senses.

Alan Millard, *Ideas For Assemblies* (Cambridge University Press: Cambridge, 1990), ISBN 0 521 38889 9, pp 35-39. Five assembly outlines.

## HABITS

'Glove Illustration' in: Bob Moffett, *Crowdmakers* (Marshall Pickering: London, 1985), ISBN 0 7208 0588 0, p 17. Object lesson.

Michael Hastings, *Addiction* (Scripture Union: London, 1988), ISBN 0 86201 387 9.

Raul Ries/Lela Gilbert, *From Fury To Freedom* (Kingsway: Eastbourne, 1988), ISBN 0 86065 543 1. Story about a drug addict.

David Day, *Why Don't You Grow Up!* (Lion Publishing: Tring, 1988), ISBN 0 7459 1334 2, pp 23-26. PSE/RE textbook with two chapters on failure and coping with it in a mature way.

# FOOD AND FEASTING

Jan Wilson, *Feasting For Festivals* (Lion Publishing: Oxford, 1990), ISBN 0 7459 1567 1. Customs and recipes to celebrate the Christian Year.

Aviva Paraïso/Jon Mayled, *Soul Cakes And Shish Kebabs* (Religious and Moral Education Press: Exeter, 1987), ISBN 0 08 035097 6. Multifaith Cookery Book.

Malvina Kinard/Janet Crisler, *Loaves & Fishes* (Keats Publishing: Connecticut, 1975), ISBN 0 87983 110 3. Cookery book with foods from Bible times.

Hubert J. Richards, *The Passover Meal* (McCrimmons: Great Wakering, 1990) ISBN 0 85597 432 X.

Lynne Scholefield, *Living Festivals: Passover* (Religious and Moral Education Press: Exeter, 1982), ISBN 0 08 027867 1.

*Enjoy The Seder At Home—Passover Part 1* (Michael Goulston Education Foundation/Pergamon Educational Productions: Exeter), ISBN 0 08 034571 9. Jewish Festival Audio Cassette.

*Living Festivals—Video 1 Passover* (Christian Education Movement/Pergamon Educational Productions: Exeter), ISBN 0 08 034542 5. Available from Chansitor Publications, St Mary's Works, St Mary's Plain, Norwich, NR3 3BH.

# IT'S A MIRACLE!

Franco Zeffirelli, *Jesus Of Nazareth* (ITC Entertainment/Bagster Video, Westbrooke House, 76 High Street, Alton Hants GU34 1EN, 1980). Video with clips of miracles performed by Jesus. A four-part film originally made for television with the much acclaimed portrayal of Jesus by Robert Powell. Filmed on location in Morocco and Tunisia.

*The Rescue Of Jessica McClure* (Odyssey Video/Interscope Productions: 1990). Available for hire in some local video shops. Ninety-one minutes.

*Jesus—The Life That Changed History* (Campus Crusade for Christ/International Films, The Coach House, 55 Drayton Green, London W13 0JD). The script of this video is taken almost entirely from Luke's Gospel (Good News Version). Filmed as far as possible in authentic locations in Israel.

Raymond Brady, *The Christian Way 1* (Veritas Publications:

Dublin, 1980), ISBN 0 86217 041 9, p 65. A Catholic RE textbook.

John Bailey (ed), *Blueprint Book Three* (Galliard/Stainer & Bell: London, 1976), ISBN 0 85249 353 3, pp 779-788. Readings.

## DON'T BLAME ME!

Dee Moss, *A Word For Your Year* (Collins Liturgical Publications: London, 1986), ISBN 0 00 599840 9, pp 55-57. Assembly outline on 'Honesty'.

Margaret Cooling, *Assemblies for Primary Schools—Summer Term* (Religious and Moral Education Press: Exeter, 1990), ISBN 0 08 040447 2, pp 33,67. Assembly outlines on 'The Lie Detector' and 'The Truth'.

Redvers Brandling, *Assembly News* (Edward Arnold: Sevenoaks, 1989), ISBN 0 7131 7739 X, pp 40-41. Reading.

W. J. Wilcock, *Through The Year—An Assembly Book For The 1990s* (Basil Blackwell: Oxford, 1990), ISBN 0 631 90466 2, pp 10-11. Assembly outline.

## GETTING TO KNOW YOU

Bob Moffett, *Power Pack* (Scripture Union: London, 1983), ISBN 0 86201 190 6. Youth group outline 3 on 'Fellowship' and 5 on 'Masks And Role Play'.

Bob Moffett, *Power Pack 2* (Scripture Union: London, 1986), ISBN 0 86201 342 9. Youth group outline 4 on 'Friendship Without Labels'.

*In The Bin* (Scripture Union, 130 City Road, London EC1V 2NJ, 1972). This twelve-minute cartoon is about Arthur Grimble who has a mask for every mood and every situation. The dustman helps him strip off his masks. Available in video or soundstrip format.

## FORGIVENESS

Robert W. Bell/D. Bruce Lockerbie, *In Peril On The Sea* (Inter-Varsity Press: Leicester, 1990), ISBN 0 85110 856 3. The true story of Robert Bell, aboard the freighter 'SS West Lashaway' when it was hit by a German U-boat torpedo, and the remarkable reunion and reconciliation forty years later with the crew of the U-boat.

Margaret Cooling, *It Makes Me Angry!* (Lion Publishing: Oxford, 1990), ISBN 0 7459 1577 9, pp 28-29. PSE/RE textbook with a chapter on 'Anger And Forgiveness'.

Margaret Cooling, *Assemblies For Primary Schools—Autumn Term*, (Religious and Moral Education Press: Exeter, 1990), ISBN 0 08 040445 6, pp 68-79. Ten assembly outlines on 'Forgiveness'.

'Forgiveness' in: Anthony P. Castle, *Quotes & Anecdotes—An Anthology For Preachers & Teachers* (Kevin Mayhew: Bury St Edmunds, 1979), ISBN 0 905725 69 7, pp 323-324.

*Under The Shadow* (Scripture Union, 130 City Road, London EC1V 2NJ, 1986). Video with three powerful and moving documentary-style programmes on themes related to forgiveness, suffering and Easter. 'The Only Son' (fourteen minutes) is a dramatic account of the murder of the son of the Bishop of Iran. 'The Dividing Wall' (twenty-two minutes) portrays two former enemies—an IRA hunger striker and a UVF paramilitary and their reconciliation as they became Christians.

## TWO-WAY COMMUNICATION

'Telephone Conversation' in: Edmund Banyard, *A Fistful Of Fivers* (National Christian Education Council: Redhill, 1989), ISBN 0 7197 0667 X, p 39. Sketch.

'Being A Good Listener' in: John Bailey (ed), *Blueprint Book Three* (Galliard/Stainer & Bell: London, 1976), ISBN 0 85249 353 3, p 962. Reading.

Tony Rousell, *Our Turn For Assembly* (Basil Blackwell: Oxford, 1985), ISBN 0 631 13664 9, pp 51-53. Assembly outline 'In Touch With Heaven'.

*A Beginner's Guide To Revolution* (Scripture Union, 130 City Road, London EC1V 2NJ, 1985). This fifteen-minute cartoon, in video or soundstrip format, is about Sidney Penge and his Head Monitor. When Sidney opens himself to God in prayer, the 'system' comes under new management and the Head Monitor is sacked.

## A TIME TO REMEMBER

Bronwen Wild, *Gatherings* (Hodder & Stoughton: London, 1987), ISBN 0 340 39763 2, pp 90-91. Reading.

Peter Curtis/Carol Smith, *Folens RE—Thinking About Living* (Folens: Dunstable, 1990), ISBN 1 85276093 1, pp 40-43. RE textbook.

'Rabbi Hugo Gryn' on video: *Stop And Think—Collective Worship For Secondary Schools* (BBC/CTVC, Beeson's Yard, Bury Lane, Rickmansworth, Herts WD3 1DS). Sequence 4.5 in which Hugo Gryn remembers an experience he had in a Nazi concentration camp.

Sister Judith Russi, *Starting Points* (Geoffrey Chapman/Cassell: London, 1991), ISBN 0 225 66634 0, pp 48-49. Assembly outline on remembering prisoners of conscience.

## HOPE

Linda Smith, *Death—The Final Journey?* (Lion Publishing: Tring, 1988), ISBN 0 7459 1336 9. PSE/RE textbook.

Jonathan Fisher, *Interface* (Lion Publishing: Tring, 1986), ISBN 0 7459 1153 6, pp 96-103. Readings: 'Death And Beyond'.

Patricia M. St John, *The Tanglewoods' Secret* (Scripture Union: London, 1971), ISBN 0 85421 880 7. Story book.

Brian Sibley, *Shadowlands* (Hodder & Stoughton: London, 1985), ISBN 0 340 38516 2, pp 140-144. Story of C. S. Lewis and the death of his wife Joy Davidman.

Donald Hilton (compiler), *A Word In Season—Prose And Verse For Use In Christian Education And Worship* (National Christian Education Council: Redhill, 1984), ISBN 0 7197 0410 3, pp 34-36. Poems.

'Tell Me There's A Heaven' on LP/Cassette/CD: Chris Rea, *The Road To Hell*. Song.

## PERSONAL VALUES

Michael Hinton, *Value Auction* (Christian Education Movement: London). Educational game.

Grahame Knox/David Lawrence, *Assembly Point* (Scripture Union: London, 1990), ISBN 0 86201 671 1, pp 30-31,34-37. Three assembly outlines.

David Day, *What's So Special...?* (Lion Publishing: Oxford, 1989), ISBN 0 7459 1365 2, pp 3-13,30-32. PSE/RE textbook.

David Downton/Mike Sandy, *Showing The Way* (Moorley's Publishing: Ilkeston, 1989), ISBN 0 86071 297 4, pp 17-18. Assembly outline on 'Becoming Stronger'.

Laszlo Tokes, *With God, For The People* (Hodder & Stoughton: London, 1991), ISBN 0 340 54152 0. In this autobiography Laszlo Tokes, the man who sparked the Romanian revolution in December 1989, tells his story of courage and determination.

## LANGUAGE LINES:

*God's Outlaw* (International Films, The Coach House, 55 Drayton Green, London W13 0JD). 16 mm film or video, duration ninety-five minutes, on the life of William Tyndale who translated and printed the Bible into English.

*John Wycliffe—The Morning Star* (International Films, The Coach House, 55 Drayton Green, London W13 0JD). 16 mm film or video, duration seventy-five minutes, on this early translator of the Bible from Latin into English.

*Bible Translation Project Book* (Bible Society, Stonehill Green, Westlea, Swindon, Wilts SN5 7DG, 1989).

Meryl Doney, *The Bible Project Book* (Hodder & Stoughton: Sevenoaks, 1987), ISBN 0 340 40883 9, pp 20-27.

Meryl Doney, *How Our Bible Came To Us* (Lion Publishing: Oxford, 1985), ISBN 0 85648 574 8, pp 10-17.

Linda Smith, *All About Living 1* (Lion Publishing: Tring, 1986), ISBN 0 7459 1160 9, pp 32-34. RE textbook with a section on 'What Is The Bible?'

## DECISIONS:

Michael Proctor, *First...The Good News* (CIO Publishing: London, 1982), ISBN 0 7151 4752 8, pp 52-53. Assembly outline on 'Decisions'.

Linda Smith/Isobel Vale, *Work And The World* (Lion Publishing: Tring, 1988), ISBN 0 7459 1267 2. PSE/RE textbook.

Margaret Cooling, *Love And Sex* (Scripture Union: London, 1989), ISBN 0 86201 392 5, pp 8-12. Youth group outlines on 'Decisions'.


## MISUNDERSTANDINGS:

Grahame Knox/David Lawrence, *Assembly Point* (Scripture Union: London, 1990), ISBN 0 86201 671 1, pp 38-39. Assembly outline.

Bob Moffett, *Crowdmakers* (Marshall Pickering: London, 1985), ISBN 0 7208 0588 0, pp 64-65. Youth group outline on misconceptions about God.

Nigel Blundell (ed), *The World's Greatest Mistakes* (Octopus Books: London, 1980), ISBN 0 7064 1128 5.


## DEAD ENDS:

Nick Aiken (compiler), *Prayers For Teenagers* (Marshall Pickering: London, 1989), ISBN 0 551 01931 X, pp 25-30. Prayers.

Jill MacKredie, *Time To Reflect...* (Partnership Press; Fareham, 1990), ISBN 0 9516436 0 6, p 68. Assembly outline.

Stuart & Brenda Blanch, *Learning Of God—Readings From Amy Carmichael* (Triangle/SPCK: London, 1985), ISBN 0 281 04184 9, p 112. Poem.

Hugh Patterson, *Time Together* (Macdonald/Religious and Moral Education Press: London, 1983), ISBN 0 356 09218 6/0 08 036036 X, pp 160-161. Assembly outline on 'Prisoners'.

John Bailey, *Themework* (Stainer & Bell: London, 1981), ISBN 0 85249 465 3, pp 109-116. Readings on 'Loneliness'.

Raymond Brady, *The Christian Way 3* (Veritas Publications: Dublin, 1983), ISBN 0 86217 099 0, pp 12-18. Catholic RE textbook with readings on 'Human Life: Alone'.

Lamentations 3:17–24. Bible reading.

*Living Through Aids* (CBN/Bagster Video, Westbrooke House, 76 High Street, Alton, Hants GU34 1EN). This thirty-minute video programme is about a man who developed Aids. It shows how he and his wife cope with it as Christians.

## SOAP:

David Porter, *User's Guide To The Media* (Inter-Varsity Press: Leicester, 1988), ISBN 0 85110 790 7, pp 20-35. A chapter on 'TV Soap Operas—Windowing The World'.

Alan MacDonald, *Films In Close-up—Getting The Most From Film And Video* (Frameworks/Inter-Varsity Press: Leicester, 1991), ISBN 0 85111 214 5. General reading plus film critiques.

Margaret Cooling, *Christianity Topic Book One* (Religious and Moral Education Press: Norwich, 1991), ISBN 0 900274 23 9, p 21. With a 'Fly On The Wall' activity.

*Joseph* (Scripture Union, 130 City Road, London EC1V 2NJ, 1988). This video tells in a set of four episodes the story of Joseph and how God had his hands on his life. Approximately twenty minutes each.

## LETTERS:

Eric Marshall/Stuart Hample, *Children's Letters To God* (Fount Paperbacks/Collins: Glasgow, 1976), ISBN 0 00 624175 1.

Margaret Cooling, *Assemblies For Primary Schools—Summer Term* (Religious and Moral Education Press: Exeter, 1990), ISBN 0 08 040447 2, pp 78-80. Three assembly outlines on Paul's way of letter-writing.

'Letter To God...' in: Adrian Plass, *Clearing Away The Rubbish* (Minstrel/Monarch Publications: Eastbourne, 1988), ISBN 1 85424 025 0, pp 102-103.

Sister Judith Russi, *Starting Points* (Geoffrey Chapman/Cassell: London, 1991), ISBN 0 225 66634 0, pp 32-36. Catholic book of quiet reflections with young people.

## IT'S A MYSTERY:

'Mysteries Of Space and Time' in: Jonathan Fisher, *Interface* (Lion Publishing: Tring, 1986), ISBN 0 7459 1153 6, pp 66-74. Reading.

Frank Cooke, *Get Together* (Longman: Harlow, 1987), ISBN 0 582 20614 6, pp 48-53,125-132,172-178. Assembly outlines: 'The Mysterious Presence', 'Resurrection Mystery' and 'You, The Universal Mystery'.

Alan Millard, *Ideas For Assemblies* (Cambridge University Press: Cambridge, 1990), ISBN 0 521 38889 9, pp 60-66. Six assembly outlines.

## JUDGING BY APPEARANCE:

Acts 10. Bible passage.

David McKee, *Tusk Tusk* (Andersen Press: London, 1978), ISBN 09 05 478 274. Picture fantasy story about relationships between groups that are 'different'. Designed for infant children but can be used for secondary pupils.

John Bailey (ed), *Blueprint Book Three* (Galliard/Stainer & Bell: London, 1976), ISBN 0 85249 353 3, pp 967-984. Readings.

Tony Castle, *Assembly Praise* (Marshall Pickering: London, 1991), ISBN 0 551 02013 X, pp 69-71. Assembly outline.

## MONEY/MONEY/MONEY:

'Should I Buy?' in: Brother Kenneth, *Youth Prayer* (Mowbray: Oxford, 1979), ISBN 0 264 66501 5, p 25. Prayer.

'Are You A Meanie?' in: Tear Fund, *A Resource Pack For Secondary Schools* (Tear Fund, 100 Church Road, Teddington, Middlesex TW11 8QE, undated). Questionnaire.

'Money, Money, Money' in: Jim Belben/Trevor Cooper, *Everyone's A Winner* (Bible Society: Swindon, 1987), ISBN 0 564 07782 8, pp 77-88. Role-play.

'Mount Mammon Money Prison' from: Frank Topping, *Voices In My Mind* (CTVC, Beeson's Yard, Bury Lane, Rickmansworth, Herts WD3 1DS). Audio-cassette. Script reproduced in: Frank Topping, *Act Your Age* (Hodder &

Stoughton: Sevenoaks, 1989), ISBN 0 340 50212 6, pp 100-102.
Veronica Williams, *Consumer Beliefs—Valued Riches* (Christian Education Movement: Derby, 1990), ISBN 1 85100 027 5, pp 7-17. PSE/RE textbook.

## TIME:

'Time' in: Gordon Bailey, *Stuff And Nonsense—A Collection Of Verse & Worse* (Lion Publishing: Oxford, 1989), ISBN 0 7459 1828 X, p 46. Poem.
Ecclesiastes 3:1-8. Biblical passage.
R. H. Lloyd, *Acts Of Worship For Assemblies—Volume Three* (Mowbray: Oxford, 1986), ISBN 0 264 67108 2, pp 92-94. Assembly outline on 'Time'.
R. H. Lloyd, *Services For Betweenagers* (Mowbray: Oxford, 1983), ISBN 0 264 66931 2, pp 74-78. Assembly outline on 'Time'.
Linda Hoy/Mike Hoy, *An Alternative Assembly Book* (Longman: Harlow, 1985), ISBN 0 582 36124 9, pp 208-214. Five assembly outlines.
Rowland Purton, *Assemblies* (Basil Blackwell: Oxford, 1979), ISBN 0 631 19740 0, pp 24-25. Two assembly outlines.
Joan Hasler, *An Assembly Collection* (Longman: Harlow, 1986), ISBN 0 582 36125 7, pp 177-180. Readings.

## WORDS/WORDS/WORDS:

'Tongue' in: Steve Turner, *Up To Date* (Hodder & Stoughton: Sevenoaks, 1983), ISBN 0 340 28712 8, p 38. Poem.
Michael Quoist, 'I Spoke, Lord' in: *Prayers Of Life* (Gill & Son: Dublin, 1963), pp 52-54. Prayer poem.
'Two Little Words' in: Glyn Jones, *Good Morning, Children!* (Edward Arnold: Leeds, 1980), ISBN 0 560 00802 3, pp 270-271. Reading.
Jan Thompson, *Reflecting* (Hodder & Stoughton: Sevenoaks, 1988), ISBN 0 340 42954 2, pp 38-42. Four assembly outlines.

## UNDER THE INFLUENCE

Michael Hastings, *Addiction* (Scripture Union: London, 1988), ISBN 0 86201 387 9. Youth group outlines.

'The Identity Of Jesus' in: Bob Moffett, *Crowdmakers* (Pickering & Inglis: London, 1985), ISBN 0 7208 0588 0, pp 87-88. Youth group outline.

'God In A Box' in: Gerard Kelly, *Rebel Without Applause* (Minstrel/Monarch: Eastbourne, 1991), ISBN 1 85424 132 X, p 54. Poem.

## PASS IT ON:

'Talk' in: Anthony P. Castle, *Quotes & Anecdotes—An Anthology For Preachers & Teachers* (Kevin Mayhew: Bury St Edmunds, 1979), ISBN 0 905725 69 7, pp 315-317.

'Spreading The Word Around A Bit' on video: *Riding Lights Theatre Company* (Lella Productions/Bagster Video, Westbrooke House, 76 High Street, Alton, Hants GU34 1EN). Seven-and-a-half-minute witty sketch about gossip, with an introduction by Eric Delve.

## WHAT'S YOUR NAME?:

Dee Moss, *A Word For Your Year* (Collins Liturgical Publications: London, 1986), ISBN 0 00 599840 9, pp 109-111. Assembly outline on 'What's In A Name?'

Margaret Cooling, *Assemblies For Primary Schools—Autumn Term* (Religious And Moral Education Press: Exeter, 1990), ISBN 0 08 040445 6, pp 46-57. Assembly outlines on each of Jesus' disciples and their names.

Sylvia Brimer, *Themes For Assembly* (Blackie: Glasgow, 1982), ISBN 0 216 91164 8, pp 73-77. Four assembly outlines on 'Names'.

Margaret Cooling, *Assemblies For Primary Schools—Summer Term* (Religious and Moral Education Press: Exeter, 1990), ISBN 0 08 040447 2, pp 51-71. Assembly outlines on the names and titles of Jesus.

## YOU ARE UNIQUE:

Dee Moss, *A Word For Your Year* (Collins Liturgical Publications: London, 1986), ISBN 0 00 599840 9, pp 42-43. Assembly outline on: 'Fingerprints'.

Roy McCloughry, *Taking Action* (Frameworks: Leicester, 1990), ISBN 0 85111 208 0. Practical guide book to making an impact in society.

'A Member Of Parliament' in: J. John/Sue Cavill, *Talking Heads* (Frameworks: Leicester, 1990), ISBN 0 85111 211 0, pp 28-37. Short interview with Simon Hughes MP.

## WHY ME?:

'The Long Silence' in: Bob Moffett, *Crowdmakers* (Marshall Pickering: London, 1985), ISBN 0 7208 0588 0, pp 121-122. Reading.

Michael Davis, *More Words For Worship* (Edward Arnold: London, 1980), ISBN 0 7131 0479 1, pp 109-113. Readings.

Peter Curtis/Carol Smith, *Thinking About Living* (Folens: Dunstable, 1990), ISBN 1 85276093 1, pp 10-13. Pictures which can be used as discussion starter.

## I BELIEVE:

Grahame Knox/David Lawrence, *Assembly Point* (Scripture Union: London, 1990), ISBN 0 86201 671 1, pp 61-66. Assembly outline on 'Our Father!?'

Linda Smith, *All About Living 1* (Lion Publishing: Tring, 1986), ISBN 0 7459 1160 9, pp 19-28. RE textbook with a section on 'Why Believe In God?' and 'Who (Or What) Is God?'

Reg Legg, *Pictures Of God* (Angel Press: East Wittering, 1988), ISBN 0 947785 27 2, pp 2-15. RE textbook.

Michael Keene, *Steps In Religious Education 2* (Hutchinson Education: London, 1986), ISBN 0 09 164601 4, pp 42-53. RE textbook on 'People At Prayer'.

Vida Barnett, 'Exploring The Concept Of God In Three Major Faiths' in: *RE Today* Vol 5, No 3, Summer 1988, ISSN 0266 77 38, pp 20-21.

Jan Thompson, *Reflecting* (Hodder & Stoughton: Sevenoaks,

1988), ISBN 0 340 42954 2, pp 107-115. Six assembly outlines on 'Beliefs'.

## COPING WITH DEATH:

Eleanor D. Gatliffe, *Death In The Classroom* (Epworth Press: London, 1988), ISBN 0 7162 0441 X. A chapter on 'Help Children Cope With Death And Dying' and suggestions for 'Death Education'.

Linda Smith, *Death—The Final Journey?* (Lion Publishing: Tring, 1988), ISBN 0 7459 1336 9. PSE/RE textbook.

Angela Wood, *Assembly Kit* (BBC/Longman: Harlow, 1991), ISBN 0 582 06783 9. Assembly material on 'Losing, Missing And Dying'.

## HARVEST:

Tony Rousell, *Our Turn For Assembly* (Basil Blackwell: Oxford, 1985), ISBN 0 631 13664 9, pp 88-100. Two assembly outlines.

Margaret Cooling, *Assemblies For Primary Schools—Autumn Term* (Religious and Moral Education Press: Exeter, 1990), ISBN 0 08 040445 6. Ten assembly outlines.

Simon Jenkins, *A World Of Difference* (Lion Publishing: Tring, 1988), ISBN 0 7459 1337 7, pp 21-26. PSE/RE textbook.

Kathy Keay, *How To Make The World Less Hungry* (Frameworks: Leicester, 1990), ISBN 0 85111 210 2. General reading.

*Together For Festivals 2* (Church House Publishing: London, 1987), ISBN 0 7151 0448 9, pp 72-77,98-122. Ideas, songs, stories and poems.

John Harris-Douglas/Michael Kindred, *To Play And Pray* (CIO Publishing: London, undated) ISBN 0 7151 0386 5, pp 28-32,52-57. Two games: 'The Harvest Journey' and 'THETA Trading Game'.

Martin Leach/Kevin Yell (compilers), *Act Justly* (Collins Liturgical Publications/CAFOD/Christian Aid: London, 1987), ISBN 0 00 599958 8. Fifteen drama sketches.

Tear Fund, *A Resource Pack For Secondary Schools* (Tear Fund: Teddington, undated).

Anne Wilkinson, *It's Not Fair!* (Christian Aid: London, 1985). Resource Pack.

CAFOD, 2 Romero Close, Stockwell Road, London SW9 9TY, Tel: 071-7337900.

Christian Aid, PO Box 100, London SE1 7RT, Tel: 071-6204444.

OXFAM, 274 Banbury Road, Oxford OX2 7DZ, Tel: 0865-311311.

Tear Fund/Tearcraft, 100 Church Road, Teddington, Middlesex TW11 8QE, Tel: 081-9779144.

Traidcraft plc, Kingsway, Gateshead NE11 0NE, Tel: 091-4910591.

World Vision, Dychurch House, 8 Abington Street, Northampton NN1 2AJ, Tel: 0604-22964.

## GOING TO WAR (REMEMBRANCE DAY):

R. H. Lloyd, *Acts Of Worship For Assemblies Volume Three* (Mowbray: Oxford, 1986), ISBN 0 264 67108 2, pp 94-96. Assembly outlines on 'Remembrance Sunday'.

David Self (ed), *The Assembly Handbook* (Hutchinson: London, 1984), ISBN 0 09 159240 2, pp 193-194. Two poems on 'Remembrance Sunday'.

Prayers and readings on Remembrance Day, war and peace:

Joan Hasler, *An Assembly Collection* (Longman: Harlow, 1986), ISBN 0 582 36125 7, pp 96-112.

John Ferguson, *Give Peace A Chance* (Gooday Publishers: East Wittering, 1988), ISBN 1 870568 07 9.

Peter D. Smith (ed), *Peace Offerings* (Stainer & Bell: London, 1986), ISBN 0 85249 632 X.

John Bailey (ed), *Blueprint Book Four* (Galliard/Stainer & Bell: London, 1976), ISBN 0 85249 354 1, pp 1231-1248.

Cornelia Lehn, *Peace Be With You* (Faith & Life Press: Newton/Kansas, 1980), ISBN 0 87303 061 3.

Robert Runcie/Basil Hume, *Prayers For Peace* (SPCK: London, 1987), ISBN 0 281 04265 9.

## CHRISTMAS:

Anne Farncombe, *The Christmas Book* (National Christian Education Council: Redhill, 1982), ISBN 0 7197 0343 3.

Redvers Brandling, *Christmas Is Coming* (Basil Blackwell: Oxford, 1985), ISBN 0 631 14147 2.

Pamela Egan (compiler), *The Christmas Road* (Church House Publishing: London, 1986), ISBN 0 7151 0440 3. Christmas Anthology.

Antony Ewens, *Living Festivals: Christmas* (Religious and Moral Education Press: Exeter, 1982), ISBN 0 08 027869 8.

*The Nativity* (Hanna Barbara Productions, distributed by International Films, The Coach House, 55 Drayton Green, London W13 0JD, 1986), ISBN 0 936817 18 6. Cartoon video of the Christmas story (VHS twenty minutes).

*Flesh And Blood* (Scripture Union: 130 City Road, London EC1V 2NJ, 1990). Video discussion starter illustrating what Christmas meant for Joseph (VHS Two sections, fifteen minutes each).

## EASTER 1—GOOD FRIDAY:

Grahame Knox/David Lawrence, *Assembly Point* (Scripture Union: London, 1990), ISBN 0 86201 671 1, pp 81-82. Assembly outline on 'The Cost Of Love'.

Derek Wensley/Brian Frost, *Celebration—Lent To Ascension Including Easter—Book 3* (Galliard/Stainer & Bell: London, 1970), ISBN 85249 110 7, pp 15-27. Assembly ideas for 'Good Friday'.

Joyce Huggett, *Approaching Easter* (Lion Publishing: Tring, 1987), ISBN 0 7459 1120 X. Poems and prayers.

*Together For Festivals—A Resource Anthology* (Church Information Office: London, 1975), ISBN 0 7151 0333 4, pp 46-89.

Michael Botting (ed), *More For All The Family* (CPAS/Kingsway: Eastbourne, 1990), ISBN 0 86065 861 9, pp 80-84. Illustrated talks for family services with good ideas which can be adapted for assemblies.

## EASTER 2—THE RESURRECTION:

Grahame Knox/David Lawrence, *Assembly Point* (Scripture Union: London, 1990), ISBN 0 86201 671 1, pp 78-80. Assembly outlines: 'Truth—Stranger Than Fiction!' and 'Would You Believe It?'

*The Jesus Programme—Cassette Five: Broadcast Ten* (House of David/Bible News: Wembley, 1978). Cassette tape on the crucifixion and resurrection.

Jill Davies, *Easter In The Orthodox & Western Traditions* (ILEA Religious Teachers' Centre/South London Multi-Faith Religious Education Centre, Kilmorie Road, London SE23, 1989). Resource Pack.

Mary Batchelor (compiler), *The Lion Easter Book* (Lion Publishing: Tring, 1987), ISBN 0 85648 945 X. Readings, activities and recipes.

Pamela Egan (compiler), *Words For Easter* (National Society/Church House Publishing: London, 1990), ISBN 0 7151 4791 9. Easter Anthology.

## ASCENSION:

'Ascension' in: Roy Morgan/Ruth Cottey et al, *Themes On The Life Of Jesus* (West Glamorgan County Council Education Department, County Hall, Cathays Park, Cardiff, CF1 3NE, undated), pp 52-53. Poems.

Michael Poole, *A Guide To Science And Belief* (Lion Publishing: Oxford, 1990), ISBN 0 7459 1909 X. General reading including sections on 'Miracles' and 'Belief and Evidence'.

Colin Chapman, *The Case For Christianity* (Lion Publishing: Tring, 1981), ISBN 0 85648 371 0, pp 111-123. General reading on verifications in history, philosophy and science.

## PENTECOST:

Gregory McCormick, *Discovering Together* (St Paul Publications: Slough, 1989), ISBN 085439 315 3, pp 115-126. Five assembly outlines.

Allan Scrivener, *Instant Art For Festivals* (Palm Tree Press: Bury St Edmunds, 1989), ISBN 0 86208 121 1, pp 31-41. Activities such as how to make Pentecost 'Helicopters'.

*Ascension And Pentecost* (Durham Diocesan Board of Education: Carter House, Pelaw Leazes Lane, Durham, DH1 1TB, undated). Theological reflections and practical ideas for infant, junior and secondary age range.

Gwyneth Windsor/John Hughes, *Jesus And The Birth Of The*

*Church* (Heinemann Educational: Oxford, 1990), ISBN 0 435 30270 1, pp 68-75. RE textbook.

Tony Castle, *Assembly Praise* (Marshall Pickering: London, 1991), ISBN 0 551 02013X, pp 155-158. Assembly outline.

Michael Botting (ed), *For All The Family* (Kingsway: Eastbourne, 1984), ISBN 0 86065 314 5, pp 103-116. Ideas for illustrated talks for family services which could be adapted for assemblies.

*Drawn Together: Resources For Broadly Christian Acts Of Worship—Over Elevens* (Christian Education Movement/Salvation Army: Derby, 1991), ISBN 1 85100 039 9, pp 47-54. Assembly material.